Avatar Of The Electric Guitar
The Genius Of Jimi Hendrix

Avatar Of The Electric Guitar
The Genius Of Jimi Hendrix

By Greg Prato

Written by Greg Prato
Printed and distributed by Greg Prato Writer, Corp
Published by Greg Prato Writer, Corp
Front cover design by Mary Prato

ISBN: 9798644612628

Introduction

"I want you to listen to this," the teacher told the student. No – I'm not talking about a frank discussion between Obi Wan Kenobi and Luke Skywalker, but rather, between yours truly and my guitar teacher at the time, circa 1983. I had been taking guitar lessons for about a year, but I suppose I was not progressing at a pace to my instructor's liking.

Perhaps sensing that I needed some inspiration, he produced a cassette tape pre-set to a strategic point – to be played on my stereo. Immediately upon the music starting, I could tell that the guitar playing sounded different than the MTV-approved heavy metal I was primarily listening to at the time. The song? "Voodoo Child (Slight Return)" by Jimi Hendrix. No doubt, I was extremely impressed.

Although I wish I could say that this sonic encounter inspired me to study guitar more seriously (it would actually take another few years for me to hunker down and focus on the ins and outs of instrument), it did inspire me to pick up Jimi's *Smash Hits* collection on cassette in the spring of '84. From that point onward, Jimi was my favorite guitarist.

In fact, for some strange reason, I can recall when I acquired my next few Hendrix albums – the *Kiss the Sky* comp on vinyl for Christmas '84, *The Essential Jimi Hendrix* double-LP set sometime in '85, and *Jimi Plays Monterey* on cassette in early '86 (followed by a budget-priced *Band of Gypsys* cassette shortly thereafter), before Old Saint Nick left me the "ultimate trio" of *Are You Experienced, Axis: Bold as Love,* and *Electric Ladyland* on CD under the Christmas tree in '89.

Much has been said about Jimi over the years, and many a book has been written – mostly from a biographical point of view. Knowing that the 50 year mark of his passing was approaching in 2020, I decided the time was "write" to pay tribute to this guitar master by putting together a book – but not akin to the majority of previous literary offerings. Instead of attempting to re-tell his life story, I thought it would be a different approach to interview a variety of well-known and respected rock guitarists, have them share their thoughts, opinions, and memories of Jimi, and compile them all together – covering a range of topics/subjects.

As a result, I believe I've created a book that offers unique insight into the legend of Jimi Hendrix, and what made him unlike any other musician before or after...all these years later.

So let us stop talking falsely now the hour's getting late,
Greg Prato

p.s. Questions? Comments? Feel free to email me at gregprato@yahoo.com.

Interviews

Adrian Belew – Frank Zappa, David Bowie & Talking Heads guitarist, King Crimson singer/guitarist, solo artist
Mick Box – Uriah Heep guitarist
Caspar Brötzmann – Caspar Brötzmann Massaker guitarist
Cheetah Chrome – Dead Boys guitarist
KK Downing – Judas Priest guitarist
Rik Emmett – Triumph singer/guitarist
Don Felder – Eagles guitarist
Scott Gorham – Thin Lizzy guitarist
Kirk Hammett – Metallica guitarist
Randy Hansen – singer/guitarist
Reverend Horton Heat – singer/guitarist
Curt Kirkwood – Meat Puppets singer/guitarist
Bruce Kulick – Kiss & Grand Funk guitarist
Paul Leary – Butthole Surfers guitarist
Alex Lifeson – Rush guitarist
Richard Lloyd – Television guitarist
Frank Marino – Mahogany Rush singer/guitarist
John Petrucci – Dream Theater guitarist
Doug Pinnick – King's X singer/bassist
Andy Powell – Wishbone Ash singer/guitarist
East Bay Ray – Dead Kennedys guitarist
Uli Jon Roth – Scorpions guitarist, solo artist
Michael Schenker – Scorpions, UFO & Michael Schenker Group guitarist
Billy Sheehan – David Lee Roth, Mr. Big & Sons of Apollo bassist
Brian Tatler – Diamond Head guitarist
Kim Thayil – Soundgarden guitarist
Ron "Bumblefoot" Thal – Guns N' Roses guitarist & Sons of Apollo guitarist, solo artist
Steve Vai – Frank Zappa, David Lee Roth & Whitesnake guitarist, solo artist
+ a few previously-published interviews that I conducted!

Chapters

Chapter 1
First Experience

The earliest memories of hearing the music of Jimi.

ULI JON ROTH [Scorpions guitarist, solo artist]: I first heard it on German television in late '66 or early '67 – I'm not 100% sure. But my dad came into my room, and said, "There's a guy playing guitar with his teeth!" And there was Jimi – I think doing "Hey Joe." It passed me by a little bit, because I was very young and I hadn't even started playing the guitar at that time. Then the next thing was really through my neighbors – my best friend – he turned me on to a lot of music back then, before I started playing. And then gradually, I heard about Jimi Hendrix.

But really the crunch point was January 1969, when I got to see a Hendrix show in Hamburg [January 11th at Musikhalle]. And that changed *everything* for me. That really turned on the big "lightbulb" in my artistic mind, and influenced me in so many ways afterwards – not just musically, but artistically, and also, spiritually, because Hendrix had a powerful spiritual message. Which more and more, I began to understand the older I got. At the beginning, it was more the music. The lyrics and all that, I listened to it later.

KK DOWNING [Judas Priest guitarist]: The first time was with his first album, *Are You Experienced.* It was an instant hit – absolutely monumental. With me and a few of my friends, it was the thing that we had all been waiting for. It literally did give everything that was happening a real kick in the backside. Not to say there wasn't great things happening – because there was – but it really was totally electrifying. And I think that all the guys that went to see Hendrix in the UK before even his album was released – because he had come to small clubs and jammed, and Clapton was there, Pete Townshend. *Everybody* was completely wowed.

I would have been 16 at the time, and I remember it well. I played the record to death. What's great was John Mayall's Blues Breakers and Cream were all around at the time, and it still was very much blues-based – even though Cream were definitely a progressive blues band. It didn't take everybody by storm, because Hendrix came over, and people had an aversion to this crazy looking black dude, doing all this weird shit. It took a while for a lot of people to get acclimated.

ANDY POWELL [Wishbone Ash singer/ guitarist]: For me, he blew into London…it was like some kind of shaman or something. He had the clothes, he had the look, he was sexy with the guitar – he was a showman. We were all following people like Peter Green and Eric Clapton, and then Hendrix blew in, and it was like, *"Whoa."* He was at one with the guitar, and he had this psychedelic thing going – the clothes and the flamboyance. He took to London – he loved going down to Carnaby Street and down to Portobello Road, and buying all the clothes. He just took it all to another level.

So, he had the whole thing wrapped up in one – the image, the clothing, the guitar, the sex. He had this attitude where he just didn't give a damn. That was really *a feeling* – it was kind of rebellious. He had this nice charm about him, as well. But I think with songs like "The Wind Cries Mary" and "Axis: Bold as Love" – those songs captivated me, because it was like soundscapes. They were aurally very addictive, but he painted these pictures with the music. And the guitar, in particular – he used the feedback and the tremolo. So, those were my early impressions of Hendrix.

FRANK MARINO [Mahogany Rush singer/ guitarist]: I first heard Jimi Hendrix before his album was released in Canada. A person that we knew had gone to England, and they came back with this record by a guy named Jimi Hendrix. I went down to this guy's basement, and he said, "You've got to hear this thing I got in England!" In those days, there was grass and stuff, so he puts the headphones on my head, and the first thing that he played me was "Are You Experienced" – with the backwards guitar. I was like, "Oh my God…*what is this*?!"

I wasn't a guitar player at the time – I was actually a drummer. But just the sound of it…I don't think I've ever had a more life-changing musical moment. Maybe you could say that the Beatles had sort of done that in a way, but that was not from the point of view of the music – it was more from the fad of when Beatlemania started, really. Or the '60s. But at that point, to hear that…that was just *so* ridiculously different.

And I remember looking at the cover and asking the guy, "Where is the fourth member of the band?" Everything about it was weird – the cover, the clothing. And it turned out to be the Jimi Hendrix

Experience. That's the first time I heard Jimi Hendrix.

BILLY SHEEHAN [David Lee Roth, Mr. Big & Sons of Apollo bassist]: When *Are You Experienced* first came out, I was getting into playing and being in bands – the whole thing started for me. I played with a couple of guys – a drummer and a guitar player – and was *so* blown away by Jimi Hendrix. It really was a life-changing thing. Suddenly, there was a focus on this guitar sound and these songs, and this guy and this voice that was like nothing else. And I loved the Beatles, the Stones, and the Yardbirds and all the bands I grew up with…but suddenly, a whole new world opened up – and it's called "Jimi Hendrix." I was very excited about it.

ALEX LIFESON [Rush guitarist]: It was the summer of 1967 and I was at [original Rush drummer] John Rutsey's house – and his brother Bill had just purchased *Are You Experienced*. He dropped the needle and "Purple Haze" played through that tiny speaker and changed our world immediately.

RANDY HANSEN [singer/guitarist]: The first time I heard it, I bought the wrong record. I was already playing guitar, and this guy at school told me…well, I carried my guitar to school one day, and the guy said, "Who do you think you are? *Jimi Hendrix?*" And I said, "Who's that?" And then he tried to tell me all about him playing Monterey and burning the guitar, and that he played the guitar in more positions than anybody ever played the guitar – he played with his teeth and all this stuff. He just informed me all about him.

And then I went out and bought the wrong record – I bought *Get That Feeling* [an album comprised of early recordings of Jimi backing singer Curtis Knight]. I came back the next day, and he said, "Did you get the record? What did you think?" "It's alright." "What do you mean it's 'alright'?! Which record did you buy?" I told him, and he goes, "You bought the wrong record! Go back and get *Are You Experienced.*" I saw that album too, but I liked the cover on *Get That Feeling*, because you can see Jimi close up. I then bought *Are You Experienced*, took it home, and it was like a total revelation.

At that point, I thought the Ventures was as far as the guitar was going to go – and the Beatles and the Stones, and all that stuff. I really thought, "That's what guitar is. That's the correct way to play it and that's all there is to it." And then I heard Jimi, and I was like, "Wait a minute...*what is going on*?"

It seemed like – at the time – that they were just starting to experiment in the studio with what the studio can do, also. Because some of the sounds that are on that record is the tape sped up twice as fast, and they would slow it down half speed and record something, and speed it back up again. And you'd hear it an octave above and twice as fast. He does that on the end of "Purple Haze." There's all kinds of things they were using. It took *years* to figure out they were doing this and that.

To me, it became an unsolvable puzzle – because Jimi's prowess as a guitar player, some of the things he pulled off...now, back in the day, people would take speed and LSD. Too much coffee will make you play a little faster than you normally would. So, you don't really know what all that is that you're hearing. You're hearing the effects of drugs, the studio, a producer, and Jimi Hendrix's wild brain. To me, just the whole thing was so impressive.

There was certain music I heard back then that I thought was magic because I couldn't tell what I was hearing. "Is that a guitar? Is that a keyboard? *What the hell is that*?!" And Jimi was loaded up with stuff like that. There's all kinds of things that are in there – there's a kazoo in "Crosstown Traffic," harpsichord in "Burning of the Midnight Lamp." People just think of Jimi as a wild guitar player, but if you really look back at what he did and the production of it...

That was in '67 – it was right when he came out actually, when "Purple Haze" was just hitting the radio. It seemed like I bought the record, and the next thing I know, "Purple Haze" is on the radio. I went, "*Wow*. This guy is catching on fast." And after his career started extending – before he died – I was convinced that he was supernatural, in a way. There was something very "supernatural" about this guy. I don't know, I used to think some musicians were ordained by God to be here. To like...save the planet. If that's true, then Jimi was the king of that – at the time he was here.

My father died when I was ten, and I didn't have a whole lot of guidance – until I started getting into Hendrix, and I started listening to his lyrics and what his dogma was. I kind of guided my life a lot by that – as if he was my father. But it's still kind of like that when I listen to what he's got to say – "Valleys of Neptune" or something like that.

7 FIRST EXPERIENCE

RICHARD LLOYD [Television guitarist]: I first heard the album *Are You Experienced* at a friend's house – in the Upper West Side of Manhattan. I had a little clique, and it centered around this fella, Danny. And we used to go over and listen. That year, a bunch of debut albums came out, and Hendrix was among them…along with Traffic and some others. I thought *Are You Experienced* was a bit *noisy*. [Laughs] My first impression was it was noisy. Y'know, when they sent Reprise the tapes, they put on the box, "DELIBERATE DISTORTION: DO NOT CORRECT."

ADRIAN BELEW [Frank Zappa, David Bowie, & Talking Heads guitarist, King Crimson singer/guitarist, solo artist]: The first Hendrix song I ever heard was "Purple Haze." The sound floored me! The opening dissonant notes with guitar and bass, the simplistic sound of the track itself with just three instruments and a voice, the tone of Jimi's voice, and in particular the sound of the guitar solo. I had no visual reference at that moment, and something in Jimi's vocal made me assume these must be older, more mature guys – maybe accomplished blues players or something. Or maybe it was the way he talked while he sang – like old blues players sometimes do.

At the time, I was in my first teen band called the Denims. We had been labeled "Cincinnati's Own Beatles" by WSAI – the most popular radio station – because we did exact copies of the early Beatles stuff. I was the drummer and singer, and very happily playing the part of Ringo – while singing the parts of John and Paul. I had just barely started teaching myself to play guitar in order to write the songs I could hear in my head.

I was living in the world of "singing pop bands" – not the world of virtuoso musicians. So when I first heard the Experience, I thought their playing was from another universe – I couldn't wrap my mind around how anyone was doing what they were doing. [Laughs] Even as a drummer, I was listening to Mitch Mitchell, and thinking, "I've never heard drumming like this before."

It was the second song on *Are You Experienced* called "Manic Depression" that got me. It was exciting, almost jazz-like drumming. He was using drum rudiments I had learned in marching band – double stroke rolls and paradiddles. Jimi stole the show of course, he was so far beyond anything I'd ever heard. The way he bent notes, the ferocity of his guitar sounds...*wow*. The guitar solo sound that's in the middle of "Purple Haze," that sound has been with me all my life. I've used that sound all my life. He did it with a device called an Octavia, but I do it with a similar 60's fuzzbox – called a Foxx Tone Machine. To this day, it's a mainstay in my box of tools – that particular guitar sound.

His guitar playing was so visual, and his voice...unbelievable. What a voice that is. Not many people talk about Jimi Hendrix's voice, but what a soulful singer he was. The way he always interrupted himself with these vocal asides – y'know, "Aw move over, baby!" I never heard anyone do that. You have to understand, at that time I was a teenager and whatever was on the radio was my world. It had been Roy Orbison, Ricky Nelson, and the Beach Boys, and then it became the Beatles and the Kinks. And then all of a sudden, it was this other thing from outer space...Jimi Hendrix.

MICK BOX [Uriah Heep guitarist]: At the time, I took a job for a year. I said to my mother, "I'm going to take this job for a year up in the city. And when I've paid off my guitar payments, I'm going to be a professional musician and shut the job in." So, at the time, I was working. And what I used to do is I would cycle seven miles there and seven miles back, so I could save on the train fare, and pay the guitar off quicker. I was focused. And on a Friday, there used to be a TV program – I think it was *Ready Steady Go!*, and Hendrix was supposed to be on there, with "Hey Joe." I had heard "Hey Joe" once before I think, and it was amazing.

So, I cycled back like a madman, so I could have my dinner, before I went out for a gig. And my mother made the dinner, I put it on my lap, I put on the TV, and Jimi came out. When he started playing with his teeth, I said, "LOOK AT THIS, MUM!" – and my dinner was on the floor. [Laughs] That was the first time I saw him actually play. He was so dynamic and had everything going for him. It was sexual with all his movements and everything, but his playing was from another planet at the time. He had *everything* – with the image and the whole lot.

RIK EMMETT [Triumph singer/guitarist]: It would have been around '66/'67. I can't remember when *Are You Experienced* came out [the album was released in Europe on May 12, 1967, and in the US on August 23rd], but it would have been around then. I was just starting high school. I was just making that transition from being somebody who played guitar because the Beatles did, to realizing that there was this whole other level of guitar playing that existed.

In my mind, I kind of think of the emergence of Hendrix in my life was right around the same time that Clapton was emerging, because of being the guy that had played with John Mayall and all that stuff. And my circle was a little bit sort of "English blues-centric," that I was aware of Jeff Beck and Jimmy Page, and the Yardbirds guys. And then here came Hendrix – kind of like a rocket. Clapton and Cream and Hendrix and the Experience – those were the albums that I remember going, "Oh boy. This is taking it to a whole other level."

BRUCE KULICK [Kiss, Grand Funk guitarist]: You're talking about my biggest guitar hero – he really meant a lot to me and connected to me emotionally from the first time I heard him. It was the *Are You Experienced* album. Paul Stanley and I used to chat about him when I joined the band. But for me, that style of playing and what he created on that first album was completely mind-blowing.

It coincided with my first stereo – which was a very cheap Lafayette, maybe 10-watt system. But the fact that I could hear incredible music and incredible guitar playing and jazzy drumming and creative effects, and then stereo ping-ponging between the speakers…I remembered *crying* the first time I heard that. Because you've got to remember, stereo was not very well-known and used at that time. So, I had that experience of the "audio magic" – but with some of the greatest music ever created. Especially featuring a guitar – which he will forever be "the top of the heap," shall I say, of being innovative, creative, and expressing music on an instrument that he made his own.

MICHAEL SCHENKER [Scorpions, UFO & Michael Schenker Group guitarist]: I was never really in the beginning a Jimi Hendrix fan. I found out much later that Jimi Hendrix had great songs out, with some incredible sounds – like "All Along the Watchtower." But I was never affected by that that much when it happened, because I was more focusing on melodic guitar – I was more a fan of Eric Clapton, Jeff Beck, Leslie West, and Jimmy Page. The melodic guitar is what I liked. But I was aware of Jimi Hendrix, of course.

I kind of started to hear things later in life – little bits and pieces of Jimi Hendrix. Like "All Along the Watchtower," with the incredible delay or reverb on there, together with the guitar playing is magical. It really is unbelievable. I don't know why I didn't notice that before – maybe because I was more into the rock music on a level of rock guitarists with a rock singer – like Jimmy Page with Robert Plant. I fell in love with that kind of stuff. And Rod Stewart with Jeff Beck. I was more fascinated with the singer sings, then the guitarist takes over and plays the lead, and then the singer starts again. That was something that I was enjoying.

DON FELDER [Eagles guitarist]: I think the first time I heard him must have been on his very first album, and then everything that came out after that just got better and better and better.

SCOTT GORHAM [Thin Lizzy guitarist]: I think I was in my car – on the Ventura Freeway – and "Hey Joe" came on, and I thought, *Who the fuck is that guy?*" I loved his tone, I loved his approach on the guitar. I was immediately in love straight off the bat with Jimi Hendrix.

CHEETAH CHROME [Dead Boys guitarist]: The first time I heard Jimi Hendrix was in junior high school, and the drummer in my first band had gotten *Are You Experienced* from his brother. So, we sat down there, listened to it, and the first time...we didn't get it. But we liked "Hey Joe," so we started playing along with it. And it was a doorway into the album. Because everything sounded so upside down – compared to the Beatles and the Stones.

BRIAN TATLER [Diamond Head guitarist]: He was on *The Lulu Show*, when he did "Hey Joe," and it's a classic clip that I've seen many times since – a black and white clip. And halfway through, he says, "We're going to stop playing this rubbish and do a song by the Cream." He name-checks the three guys, and off they go into "Sunshine of Your Love." And then halfway through, he says, "We're being put off the air!" It was probably a Saturday evening in the UK – prime family viewing.

But I didn't really know what to make of him – I'd probably only be a young kid, and I hadn't started playing guitar. But it definitely had some kind of an effect. And then later on, I listened to things like "Purple Haze" and "All Along the Watchtower." I remember getting a live album of his – which had "Red House" on it – and I really liked that. But probably some years after he died, when I started playing guitar did I appreciate what he had created, and the legacy that Hendrix had left.

STEVE VAI [Frank Zappa, David Lee Roth & Whitesnake guitarist, solo artist]: I remember pretty distinctly – I was ten years old and my sister had an 8-track of *Woodstock*. It was broken, and would only play one channel. And that channel happened to have on it Sly and the Family Stone performing "Dance to the Music" and Jimi Hendrix doing "The Star-Spangled Banner." And I listened to it over and over and over again. I couldn't believe that those sounds were a guitar. Not that I knew much about what a guitar could do.

So, my introduction to the guitar was, "It could make sounds like *this*." I came into the world – like many people – starting out where many great guitar players were hovering at a particular time, so a ten year old kid, who's listening to people like Hendrix and Jeff Beck and Jimmy Page, you believe, "Well...*this is where it's at*." That's kind of like your introduction.

But shortly after that, my brother got a cassette of *Are You Experienced*. And that really captured me. There was something about it that was so different than any of that other '60s music. It had a quality of invention in it, but it had imagination that seemed to be emanating from a different dimension than those other bands that were coming into our house on records and cassettes. So, that's right around the time I started playing the guitar. And basically, *meditated* to that album.

And when I started playing guitar, I was

taking lessons from Joe Satriani. I was about 12/13 years old, and he was *really* into Hendrix. So, that's where I really started to hear that body of Jimi's work – because Joe gave me *Axis: Bold as Love*, *Electric Ladyland*, and *Cry of Love*. These were really the only records available of Jimi at the time. And there was *Band of Gypsys* that had a tremendous impact on me. I listened to "Machine Gun" endlessly – *that's* where I knew I wanted to go. Or at least incorporate elements of that into my guitar playing.

DOUG PINNICK [King's X singer/bassist]: I was 16 when "Purple Haze" came out. I remember at school, I had never listened to rock music, really. There was no Led Zeppelin or anything at that point. So, I'm listening to Motown, Stax – all the soul music. After basketball games and football games, we would go to the rec room, and all of us black kids would bring our records and play music so we could dance.

And all the white kids would show up with their records…but the black kids would take the white kids' records off and put the black music on, and everybody would dance. I remember that there would always be some white kids that would be playing songs, because I would be the second one there – to get my music on, so I could dance. Because I loved to dance. And I walked into the rec room and heard this song, "Purple Haze," and went, *"What is that?"* And…I went over, took it off, put my music on, and started dancing. [Laughs]

I remember hearing bits and pieces about Jimi Hendrix in the media. I lived in Chicago, and there really weren't rock magazines that I read. I think maybe we had *Rolling Stone*, but I never read it. The first rock record I ever bought was *Led Zeppelin II* – and that was in '72. So, '72 is when I started getting into rock music, and I had come across a couple of Jimi Hendrix records, and said, "I want to get into him." But I *still* couldn't get into him. It just didn't make sense to me – my mind wasn't open.

I was on the road with a show group that did choreography and stuff, and that's when I started reading rock magazines, and that's when I read that Jimi Hendrix had died. I was sad about it. I remember driving in the van – going to Arizona, or something – and I stopped at this music store and bought a cassette of *Cry of Love*, because I wanted to get into it, and to see, "Well, what did I miss?"

I played *Cry of Love*, and I'm going, "Wow…I like this record!" I wasn't crazy about it, but I was digging it. And then, I listened to *Band of Gypsys*, and I go, "Alright. This is *exactly* what I've been looking for all my life." Buddy Miles was one of my favorite singers and drummers at the time, and I had been listening to Buddy Miles. So, when he got together with him and Billy Cox, and it was a three-piece, all-black rock band, it was something that I really related to. There's a way that black people play – a couple of nuances. There's things that we do that white people don't do, because they just don't come from our culture. And they had that, and I've always looked for that in a rock band. So, I felt really at home.

And also, I had just started playing bass. So, that was one of the records I learned how to play bass to. I know that record backwards and forwards. And playing bass left-handed – and I looked like him back in the day – I didn't sing like him, until…I don't know what happened. I didn't really sound like him when I sang, until later on in my life, when I started just naturally singing and it sounded like him. And people were going, "Man, you sound like Hendrix." But then when I started hearing myself back, I was like, "Oh wow…you are doing that 'Bob Dylan-type thing' – sliding up your notes."

But after that, I started doing Hendrix covers – to the point that I did a solo Jimi Hendrix record [2018's *Tribute to Jimi (Often Imitated But Never Duplicated)*]. And I *really* studied him – and still study him. And doing the Experience Hendrix Tour [in 2019] and doing Hendrix songs, I got to really channel him and really learn his inflections and learn how to sound just like him. I used to sound like him just naturally, but I can turn it on now.

KIM THAYIL [Soundgarden guitarist]: Because of my age, my initial impression of Hendrix was hearing he had passed away in my *Weekly Reader* – remember those *Scholastic* newsletters that used to go out once a week to grade school kids? I believe I was in 6th grade and there was a news article about the death of Jimi Hendrix. I think it also mentioned Janis Joplin and somebody else…maybe Jim Morrison, I don't know. I remember I wasn't that acquainted with him – I don't think I knew any of his songs. I was a grade school kid and into top-40 radio. So, the name "Jimi Hendrix" didn't ring a bell – I didn't have any older brothers and my parents were immigrants, so there was no clear reference point.

When I finally did hear him on FM/AOR radio, I heard the songs "Foxy Lady" and "Fire."

What did I think when I first heard it? I thought it was heavy, which I had an inclination for – I liked the heavier/faster songs by the Beatles, Elton John, Three Dog Night or whoever back then. So, when I heard Hendrix, it was the same thing – it had guitar and it was heavy, but it was darker. I remember getting a feeling that it was a little bit darker and a little more psychedelic.

Similar to the feeling I got when I first heard Black Sabbath's "Paranoid" – which was also around 6th grade. Both those artists had *a darkness* in it – in both the production and the way it was written. But not in the case with "Fire" – "Fire" seemed like a very fast, funky, visceral energetic rock song. But in the case of "Purple Haze" and "Foxy Lady" it had a darkness in the guitar tone.

REVEREND HORTON HEAT [singer/guitarist]: I'm pretty sure it was hanging around a friend of mine's house. I was the oldest child in my family, but there were other boys in the neighborhood that had older brothers and sisters – that had all the cool albums. So, it was at a friend of mine's house. He had his brother's albums playing – Deep Purple and Jimi Hendrix. It was really cool – it was a real eye-opener. And then when I started playing guitar, I really gathered a larger appreciation for Jimi Hendrix. Which would have been only a couple of years after he died was when I first started playing guitar. So, like '72/'73/'74 – something like that.

There was another guitar player going around that time that I was getting interested in. I was kind of a "blues kid" in a way. There was this guitar player, Roy Buchanan, and he had a song that was getting airplay a lot on our local rock station – he did a version of "Hey Joe." And it was right around that point I realized, "Hey, that's a Hendrix song." You've got to remember – I was still a kid. But just his sound and his way of playing – it was right up my alley.

PAUL LEARY [Butthole Surfers guitarist]: I would have been in high school. Up to that point in my life, I had been a big Beatles fan – it was almost difficult liking anything outside of the Beatles when I was really young, and Jimi Hendrix was one of the first people to kind of bitch-slap me into realizing there is a lot of good music out there. I can remember even through high school – I graduated high school in '75 – they allowed students to bring in records and play music during lunch in the cafeteria. And it was always Hendrix, Black Sabbath, and ZZ Top.

EAST BAY RAY [Dead Kennedys guitarist]: Some of the older kids in the neighborhood had it. I remember somebody was playing it, and like, "Wow...this is great!" The first LP – *Are You Experienced.* For some odd reason, I was kind of behind the times. In the early '70s, I didn't really like music that much. So I started going back into the '60s, and started discovering the Pink Floyd and Jimi Hendrix records, and that's what I was listening to in the early '70s. Again, I think both of them put the little hairs on the back of my neck on end. And they both had the psychedelic sound – which was an influence and you can hear in some of the Dead Kennedys songs.

19 FIRST EXPERIENCE

CURT KIRKWOOD [Meat Puppets singer/ guitarist]:   Derrick [Bostrom, Meat Puppets' drummer] had a friend named Jack Knetzger. Jack and Derrick played quite a bit and I met Jack the same night I met Derrick. But Jack was *way* into Jimi and he kind of played like him – he played a Stratocaster and was just out of his mind. He was a good guitar player – a lot of fun. Pretty basic, but could play psychedelic jams. Derrick had some of those records, I think.

I never had a Jimi Hendrix record until later. Hanging out with Derrick and Jack and just becoming a little bit less of a "westside Phoenix guy." Westside Phoenix was more about Deep Purple and Led Zeppelin – more of the stuff you would hear on the radio. Hendrix was gone by the time I was a teenager…I mean, you would hear it – but FM radio was playing what was going on in the '70s more.

CASPAR BRÖTZMANN [Caspar Brötzmann Massaker guitarist]:   If my remembrance is not foxing me, my first listen to Jimi Hendrix was the record called *Smash Hits*. I was somewhere around 16 years old in the mid-70's. I already played guitar and was a fan of Led Zeppelin and Deep Purple. I am sorry to say this, but my first initial impression was that I didn't like the music of Jimi Hendrix and was asking myself, "Where are the guitar solos like Jimmy Page and Richie Blackmore I am looking for?" I remember the guitar intro of "Hey Joe" with the empty high E-string was interesting.

This all began to change around a year later, when I had listened to the intro of "Wild Thing" at the Monterey Pop Festival with this uncommon guitar sound of feedback. The night of a burning guitar had started to conquer and inspire my guitar playing. After I had listened to Monterey, I bought the record *War Heroes* and listened to this song called "Midnight." At this moment I guess I began to be a fan of Jimi Hendrix. I didn't comprehend or understand in this moment, that I had met the master of my heroes.

RON "BUMBLEFOOT" THAL [Guns N' Roses guitarist & Sons of Apollo guitarist, solo artist]: I first heard Jimi when I was about ten years old, and it was that "best of" album [1969's *Smash Hits*], and the first songs I learned were "Purple Haze," "Foxy Lady," and "All Along the Watchtower." I remember sitting at home and dropping the needle over and over on that. I got the beginning of [sings beginning of "All Along the Watchtower"], but right before the second verse when he did that fast run...just trying to get the exact choice of notes on that pentatonic riff that he was doing – the faster one.

KIRK HAMMETT [Metallica guitarist]: The first time I heard Jimi Hendrix, I was too young to figure out how old I was! [Laughs] Because my older brother – who's eleven years older than me – had the first three albums. I distinctly remember *Are You Experienced* and *Axis* – because of the album covers. And being a kid, I was trying to figure out the album covers – because of the imagery. I would sit there and stare at them while the music was going on. I think I was maybe five or six years old. I remember looking at *Are You Experienced* and looking at Jimi's jacket, and thinking, "This is really exotic looking." And then looking at the *Axis* cover, and seeing all the multiple faces, and seeing those exotic creatures, as well – it actually is a Hindu image.

Fast-forward maybe seven or eight years, I remember sitting with my friends and I was at the third concert I'd ever been to – Led Zeppelin at Day on the Green in 1977. Judas Priest opened the show and Rick Derringer played…and then there was a *long* wait before Led Zeppelin came on. And the reason for that wait was because John Bonham got in a huge fight with Bill Graham's security guards backstage and the cops came. There was a huge issue – and there was some contention on whether Led Zeppelin should go on or not. It was literally, like, 90 minutes…which is not cool – for *any* band. [Laughs]

But in that 90 minutes, I remember sitting there, and they were playing songs over the PA. And this one song came on, and I was like, "I KNOW THAT SONG!" I was looking around to see if anyone else knew it. I said to my friend's older brother – who was responsible for taking me and my friend to see Led Zeppelin in the first place, because he was 18 or 19 years old – "Who is this?" And he said, "*'Purple Haze' by Jimi Hendrix, man.*" The last time I'd heard that song I was five or six years old.

After the Led Zeppelin concert, I went out and bought *Are You Experienced* and *Woodstock.* I was fourteen years old. It was like…*a realization.* I was already pursuing my own taste – my own musical aesthetic at that point. And Jimi Hendrix fell right into the middle of that aesthetic – which was a leaning towards hard rock. Y'know, Led Zeppelin, Deep Purple, Black Sabbath, Aerosmith – that kind of stuff. So, Jimi Hendrix is right in there. Theoretically, you can say "Purple Haze" was one of the first songs I'd ever heard.

And I'll tell you, you know what I reacted to most? *The tone of the guitar.* Just that fuzzed out Strat through a Marshall sound – it really got to me. And also, the intro [sings the opening guitar part]…that's *so* evil! But when I played it on the guitar – when I first started playing guitar – "Purple Haze" was the first song I ever learned how to play. But I could never get that octave at the very top *right*. It never sounded right…until I figured out that I was playing the bass part, and what Jimi Hendrix played was the flatted fifth. You can say that the top of the measure – the A-sharp octave for the bass – Jimi is playing the E note, underneath that A-sharp, which creates a real, real evil sound.

When I realized that, I thought, "This is the key to that sound that Black Sabbath uses, that Deep Purple uses, that all these blues bands use…it's that flatted fifth! It's that 'blues note' that's in the pentatonic scale." Some of the first music theory that I had ever been exposed to was from that song. Also, the E7 sharp 9 – the chord that Jimi Hendrix used for "Purple Haze," "Foxy Lady," and tons of other songs – that's a really complicated chord for someone who was just starting to learn how to play guitar…but I managed to play it.

And so, I learned how to play "Purple Haze" – and I learned it completely wrong. But that's just what happens when you're first learning how to play guitar. I remember going to school the next day and saying to my friends, "I think I can play 'Purple Haze' now…we should form a band!" And literally, we were like, "OK. *You're* going to be the drummer, *you're* going to be the bass player, *you're* going to be the singer, and *I'm* going to be the guitar player." And at the end of the week, we showed up at my friend's house.

We borrowed a Vox amp from the high school music class – and we *all* played through it. It had four inputs, so we could plug in bass, guitar, and vocals. We turned it up…and that amp lasted about three minutes before we blew it up. [Laughs] But you know what? We *still* kept on playing through it. I played "Purple Haze" every day for the next three months – trying to get it better and better, and trying to do the solo. Bit by bit, I would get a note here, a phrase there, get some rhythm things here. And I started branching out on other songs on *Are You Experienced* that were in my skillset – *before* Jimi started getting more sophisticated in his chords and his structures and his harmonies and his textures.

It was just a perfect primer for me.

Chapter 2
In Concert

Those lucky to have seen Jimi live on stage share their memories.

ANDY POWELL: I saw two of his early shows when he came to England. One was playing at the Royal Festival Hall [on September 25, 1967] – which was a very staid, "classical" kind of venue in London. And then I saw him play at one of the early festivals – the Woburn Music Festival at Woburn Abbey [on July 6, 1968]. I guess I must have been about 16 or 17.

I liked his sense of humor on stage. I'll never forget when at the Royal Festival Hall show, it was kind of a sedate audience. Everyone was very reverential towards guitar players in those days – like, they'd clap at the end of a solo. And after one song, this young girl got up – I guess she wanted to move seats in the auditorium. It was a seated venue – largely used for classical music. And she walked down the steps…actually, I think she was going to the bathroom. [Laughs]

And as she walked down, she was sashaying down the stairs, Jimi got on the wah wah pedal, and he actually – as she took a step – was going, "Wah-wa-wah-wa-wah." He created this really comedic version of her hip movements on the stairs. He had this cartoon mind. He picked up on the movement that she was making. And she picked up on it and the audience picked up on it – we all laughed. It was just a wonderful moment and I'll never forget it. That was his kind of cheeky sense of humor. And I think that endeared him to the London audiences. He was spontaneous.

KK DOWNING: I don't think it was until his first tour of the UK – I think it was the first tour. I was born in '51, so in '67, I would have been 16. I got to see him on that tour a couple of times – in Coventry [November 19, 1967 at the Coventry Theatre] and in Bristol [November 24, 1967 at Colston Hall]. The first two shows were *monumental*. I went to the Coventry Theatre on a train, and we didn't buy a ticket. It was one of those things – in those days, you thought you could get away with it. We'd just open up the fire exits, because we didn't have any money.

But I got to see the concert, and it was the one where he was headlining, and Pink Floyd were on there, and the Move and the Nice. I remember it well. It was all of that...in one night! It was quite amazing, really. Blown away. And then it was about a week later that I went to Bristol, and I remember sitting on the train, got into the concert, and was just an absolute fan.

But the thing is, Hendrix was a *dangerous show* at the time. I remember it, because the first show I saw in '67, people literally jumped from the balconies and stormed the stage...and I was one of them! It was just a "thing" back then. And this happened to me in Priest later on at a couple of gigs – Manchester, I remember. Back in the day, my friends would storm the stage. And it happened with Hendrix, because his show was *so* electrifying.

People just went crazy, because he came on and he had his back to the audience...and everybody was waiting for this moment to see this guy. He comes on with his back to us, he's holding that note – going into "Foxy Lady" – turns 'round, starts throwing shapes, and people were just going crazy. It was the best thing – and still is, today. I haven't seen anything that had more of an impact on me for an on-stage performer. It's not to say people didn't get hurt – but that was part of it.

So, when I went to Bristol, they opened with "Sgt. Pepper's Lonely Hearts Club Band," and it didn't get the same response. I don't know if it was Hendrix's way of "toning it down," but it was still great to see him again, because later on, it changed. People like me, who witnessed all of these live performances, did notice a change, and we understood why the change happened. A lot of people probably don't have an awareness of what went on. But it certainly did go on.

RIK EMMETT: I recall going to see him once – at the Canadian National Exhibition [on February 24, 1968]. And the sound in the place was horrible. I think this was back in the days when...I don't want to be held to account on this, but I seem to recall he had stacks of I think Sunn amps or something like that, and I don't think they were mic'd. It was still the time when guys were relying on their stacks to fill the space. And any soundman will tell you – if the sound coming off the stage is ungainly, it creates issues. And I think the PA was underpowered and undersized for the venue, and the stage level was frightening. So, that's my memory of it.

First of all, you're seeing someone who has already become iconic – in a "guitar hero" kind of sense. So, just to be in the presence of that is a wonderful and amazing kind of thing. It had its own transcendent quality to it. But, I do remember him leaning on that whammy bar, and the thing would be out of tune. This was before the time of bands figuring out that a set is *a show* – and you've got to go from song to song to song, and make it all tell a story. It seemed to me that there were breaks between songs, and re-tuning, they'd amble on stage and would take their time getting ready to play their first song. It was stuff like that – that was "of the period." It had that kind of counterculture "Hey...*we're just hippies doing our thing.*"

I was pretty young – in tenth or eleventh grade. There was an awful lot of dope smoke. [Laughs] I remember that, thinking, "Wow...I'm getting a secondhand/contact high." As for his playing, he was a revolutionary kind of player in any case. So, to witness a guy take off on these long excursions of blues jamming – which was part and parcel of what bands did in those days – it was pretty cool. You were supposed to go with it. So, it was like tripping.

BILLY SHEEHAN: So, me and the guitar player that I was playing with at the time wanted to go down to the see the show – Soft Machine opening up for Jimi Hendrix at the Buffalo War Memorial Auditorium [on March 23, 1968]. We didn't have a ride, so we thought we would take a bus, but it was late and there were no buses running – we were running down the street, trying to get downtown. By the time we got one bus we weren't sure where it took us. We were just kids from the suburbs – we had no idea where we were. We were deep in the heart of

Downtown Buffalo. Which is *not* what it is today –
it was dangerous and tough.

But we got down there and walked in just as
Soft Machine was playing and they had a screen that
went from top to bottom of the Aud. A huge, giant
screen, that they projected these amoeba-like shapes
on. We didn't know anything about drugs…but there
was a funny smell in the air. People were smoking
dope – but we didn't know what the smell was. Soft
Machine played, and we thought, "That's pretty
amazing." Then Hendrix comes out and the place
goes berserk.

And Jimi kind of stands on the base of the mic
stand and is singing the opening song, "Fire." We're
all thinking, "Jimi…what's wrong? Go nuts! *Do
something!*" And then when he sings, "Oh, move
over Rover, and let Jimi take over," he jumps back
from the mic stand, puts the guitar in his crotch, plays
[sings guitar solo], and the whole place goes crazy.
That was the first time I had ever witnessed *a rock
show*. The next day, things didn't even look the same
to me – it was like a whole other world after seeing
Jimi play. It was just mind-blowing. I became so
enamored with him and his records. But watching
him perform was the thing that really pushed it over
the edge for me. At that point, I knew where I wanted
to go and I knew what I had to do.

ADRIAN BELEW: I saw him play at the Xavier
University Fieldhouse at the University of Cincinnati
[on March 28, 1968]. He did two shows and I went
early enough to hear the first show from outside of
the building. I was disappointed that for the second
show he had cut out "Little Wing" – always one of

my favorite Hendrix songs. But when Jimi Hendrix came out and started playing, it was life-changing stuff. What stood out live was his control of feedback, the intensity of his playing, the massive sound (so loud) and more than anything: his feel. The way Jimi bent notes was unusually strong – partly because his was left-handed.

His performance was incredible. He played the guitar behind his back, and it was like watching a man trying to get a wild animal off his back. He had complete control of it...but he was trying to get it off of his back. [Laughs] He played guitar with his teeth, between his legs, he did everything with the guitar but eat it! That performance was something I wasn't prepared for. I had absorbed the records day in and day out, but the physicality of his performance, the sexuality that came from him personally – his charisma – blew me away.

Jimi Hendrix was a different package as a performer than anyone else I've ever seen. His strength was his sexuality and confidence and the way that came through his instrument and his voice. Who else has ever been that sexy with a guitar? Or any instrument, for that matter. I mean, imagine trying to do that with a tuba. [Laughs]

FRANK MARINO: A lot of my career has had that name attached to it – Jimi Hendrix. Call it for better or for worse. But my career basically started as, "This guy is a Jimi Hendrix clone." That's basically what they said about me for many, many years. And the funny part about that story is that I did see Jimi Hendrix live in 1968 [on April 2nd, at the Paul Sauvé Arena in Montreal]. But I wasn't yet a guitar player

– I only started playing guitar at the end of that year.

I had gone to this concert to see a band that was opening for him – called the Soft Machine. Being a drummer, I liked the idea that the Soft Machine's drummer did long drum solos, and I also liked Jimi Hendrix's drummer, which was Mitch Mitchell. I liked Hendrix's music by then, but it was because I liked the drumming more than I liked the guitar. It was the sound of the band – it wasn't really about guitar, it was about *the band*. So, I go to see the concert, and after the Soft Machine finished, I remember they changed the bands, and in those days, the house lights were on when the band walked on. It wasn't like how shows are today. It was in this hockey arena, and basically, some guy walks off and another guy walks on. It was really weird.

So, this guy walks out, and all I can remember at the time was, "Wait…this guy is wearing *bright red pants*." Then they start playing, but all I could hear was noise. With the echo of the room and it being very loud, you couldn't tell anything that the guy was playing. It was like it was underwater. And I couldn't hear the drummer. So, I told my brother – who had gone with me – "Eh, this is terrible. I'm going home." And I left!

I'll never forget that when I left, you know when you walk out in a hockey arena, there's concession stands, right? You can buy drinks and hotdogs and stuff. And I remember walking past the concession stands, and there was absolutely *nobody* there. Everybody was inside watching – including the people who worked! If I wanted, I could have walked up and taken food. And I was the only person walking out. The funny thing about that is that I came to be associated with that guy's name, and it's like I used to tell myself when I would hear it day after day after day, "Y'know, it's like the guy is saying, '*You will never forget my name for walking out*'!" [Laughs] So yeah, I saw him live for about five minutes – and left.

I play gigs now, so I understand what the audience was hearing at the time. If you were to go to a show for a loud band, but in a very echo-ish room...let's say you go to the soundcheck. At soundcheck, sometimes I have to go out to the console when the PA is not on, to hear what's going on, and I just hear this warble going on in the room. You hear the drummer's sizzle from the cymbals, and it's just a mish-mash. *That's* the sound that I heard.

Because they didn't exactly have a giant PA in these places – they basically had the equipment of what would have been vocal columns on the two sides of the stage. It wasn't like a PA system with giant speakers and all that. Imagine taking a band that had just played a gymnasium, and sticking them in a hockey arena with the same equipment. So, that was basically the noise, and I couldn't even tell what the drummer was playing – let alone the guitar.

If I were standing right beside the stage, I might have been able to hear what they were playing, but from back where I was...and the place was packed. It was full. Everybody was in there – it was as if it was a holy experience or something! For me, it was like, "OK...*what's this all about?*"

BRUCE KULICK: The first time I saw him I'm pretty sure would have been Madison Square Garden

– and I actually brought a portable tape recorder. You've got to remember that it wasn't so strict back then with things like this. It was a gig on May 18, 1969 – but that's where he met Buddy Miles, I'd imagine, because Buddy Miles' band opened for Hendrix. And it was a concert in the round – so it was a revolving stage. If you hear any audio of the entire concert, it's probably from my tape!

I never actually uploaded it, but I did give it to Eddie Kramer years ago – during the ending in my Kiss years. He got it to the family, and he got me a copy of another version that was from a different place in the Garden. But I know that he did digitally clean up mine – we transferred it to a DAT tape and preserved it, and it's part of the Hendrix archives. I was kind of proud to get away with that. They were three-and-a-half-inch tapes – these little guys – and it was a battery-operated UHER, which is a German brand tape recorder that I borrowed from a friend and brought it in.

What's super-fascinating about it is being in the round had some serious drawbacks, because obviously, everything was kind of primitive on stage back then. So, big Marshall stacks and the drum kit…who knows what the PA was back in '69? But the magic though is the fact that he's constantly moving – slowly revolving – the Marshall is filling the arena, but very echoey, because of the nature of it. And my microphone was in front of me, but it's picking up what my ears would have heard – which means there's way too much "hall ambience" on the band. But, think about the revolving stage – as it's getting closer to him being in direct line with me in my seat holding that microphone.

Now, that Marshall amp sounds like you're actually the microphone on top of the speaker. So, for like, three to four seconds, all the ambience is gone, and he is in your face – like, *incredibly* powerful tone. Just the nature of the physics of him performing that way, and that I captured it, I never timed how long it took for the revolution of the stage to go around – but it was a lot longer than I wanted, because the guitar sounds that would happen when he got up close, it would be like, "Oh my God! *Listen to this*!" And then all of a sudden, it goes off into the big, cavernous kind of sound again. It's been burned in my memory as an incredibly fascinating accomplishment – for me to actually capture it and experience it.

And I had good seats – they would have been where if there is a basketball game, it was where the sportscasters set up. It wasn't like a box up at the top. It was at a good level. Because let's face it – being on the floor might not have been as good as where I was. I was kind of more in the middle of the height of the arena. He played *incredible* that night. He was an artist that had his good and bad nights – even though his bad nights were still incredible.

Well, you're full tilt in the "hippie cultural years." [In response to the question, "How would you describe the atmosphere of seeing Hendrix live at Madison Square Garden?"] Think about what's happening in the pop culture and music and the Vietnam War. There's *so many* things going on. It was kind of "hippie land" – people walking around, probably smoking joints in there. And following the stage – I remember there were at least a few hundred people that would just keep walking and following him. Which was really weird. It wasn't uncommon to see bands at the Garden then – I saw Led Zeppelin in '73 or '75. *All* the acts played there. But I'm glad I made that trek – I was only 15 then. And that was pretty amazing.

DON FELDER: I actually saw him perform live at Woodstock, along with everybody else that was there – Janis Joplin, the Grateful Dead, Santana...on and on. But he actually stood out – heads and above. The energy off his stage was unbelievable. I remember seeing Crosby, Stills, Nash & Young – which I didn't know my old high school buddy, Stephen Stills, was going to be at Woodstock. And all of a sudden...there he was on stage! Seeing that kind of gave me some hope – "If he can do it, *I* can do it, too." That and the amount of rain and mud and hard conditions.

We took this nineteen fifty-something Travelall – which was a predecessor to a Suburban. We had a big mattress, and along the way, we bought some groceries and food and bottles of water, put them in that Travelall, and parked really close to the entrance of Woodstock. So, when it got really bad, we could go back and get in this Travelall, and let some storms and rain go by. I think we missed a few acts because we were in the Travelall, but in the long run, over three solid days of music, it turned out to be a smart thing – we had food, water, and shelter.

BRUCE KULICK: I bought tickets immediately [when Jimi was playing with Band of Gypsys at the Fillmore East on New Year's Eve, 1969]. Back then, things were primitive too in the way you heard about concerts – there was no instant thing on your phone or phones in your pocket. I found two tickets – I don't even remember who I went with – but I knew I should go to the early show, because I was still young. I would have been 16. I remember buying the tickets, and they were almost towards the back of the lower level – so that would have been under the balcony.

I'd been to the Fillmore East quite often, so I knew how to buy the tickets. I couldn't tell you if I would go there to the box office and buy them, but I saw *so many* bands during those years at the Fillmore. Music was so important to me. I lived in Queens, so it wasn't impossible to get to Manhattan by train. But probably the same way I got to see Derek and the Dominos – a lot of people didn't know it was Eric Clapton at first.

I probably was able to score the tickets because it was "Band of Gypsys" rather than "Jimi Hendrix." But I just knew I had to go and I went. I remember yes, it's a smaller venue – although I saw *so many* other amazing artists at the Fillmore. Bands like Mountain. And I even one time went to see the Grateful Dead – just because I wanted to see "What's this all about?" kind of thing. I saw Santana, ELP, and a lot of other really interesting bands – like, Miles Davis would be on the bill with an artist I wanted to see.

But having Hendrix there and knowing it was going to be a little different, the second it started, and I saw a completely different trio…I was aware of Buddy Miles, and always thought he was a tremendous drummer. And he sings – Mitch Mitchell didn't do any lead singing. And I heard about the bass player, Billy Cox, being his army buddy. And as a trio, Hendrix just shines, because he's such a prolific guitarist, that he could really fill all the landscapes of rhythm, lead, and singing.

Now, he's got Buddy Miles singing as well with him, and the material that I heard, I knew it was different and some of it was fresh, but I was just completely blown away with the guitar tone. His stacks were on the side of the stage where my seats were facing, so I just remember "I'm here, that's my guitar hero in front of me. This is unbelievable. I will *never* forget this." And I can still see myself in that seat, watching in awe and knowing what I was seeing was very special.

The original *Band of Gypsys* album, I knew it wasn't necessarily the performance I saw – I forgot that he did two nights, so a total of four performances. But I knew which one I went to and it was the very first one [the first of two shows on December 31, 1969]. So, years later, for them to have Eddie Kramer remix and remaster that performance – and then offer it on vinyl and CD [2019's *Songs for Groovy Children: The Fillmore East Concerts*] – and I got a chance to listen to it. And I'm so glad I got the vinyl. I listened to it with my wife, and it's just thrilling to think all these years later now – over 50 years later – this is still valid, powerful, and important.

And I was at that very screwed up event that he did for peace or something – it was at the Garden and there were many artists there [on January 28, 1970, dubbed "Winter Festival for Peace"]. I went with my high school girlfriend, and it was very late when he finally came out – and he only played a song or two. He completed just two songs – it went *so* late, this concert. And it was actually my high school girlfriend that reminded me that the subways used to close at a certain hour in New York back then – so we had to take a cab back to Queens.

But it was very disappointing. It went from 8:00 to 1:00, and it had Harry Belafonte, Blood Sweat and Tears, Dave Brubeck, Peter Paul and Mary, the Cast of *Hair*, Judy Collins…and Jimi Hendrix and his Band of Gypsys. And I'm not saying I didn't like Blood Sweat and Tears, and I was a peacenik back then, too, but come on – I was there to see *Hendrix*! So, I'm pretty damn disappointed.

Knowing that I saw Jimi and Led Zeppelin there made me especially honored and freaked out about performing at that venue [later with Kiss]. Madison Square Garden is world famous, but as a New Yorker, you know that is the premier venue to perform at. Yeah, years before, the Beatles playing Shea Stadium – of course that's exciting when you're playing a stadium. But your usual touring huge artists are going to do the Garden. It's *still* iconic. And I was quite honored – I know I invited a lot of my friends and family to see that first time we played there, which would have been on the *Asylum* tour [on December 16, 1985].

RANDY HANSEN: I saw him at Sick's Stadium here in Seattle – his last show in his hometown [on July 26, 1970]. The band that was on before them was Cactus, and they kicked major ass up there, and I thought, "How does *anybody* follow that?" So, I got up real close to the stage for when Jimi came on, and it started raining. And I thought, "This could be miserable for him. This is probably going to be not that good." And he went out there…and just kicked everyone's ass! Things were flying – just the sounds and everything. You're going, "Why does he sound different than everybody else? I don't get it." I was really blown away by it.

But not only that – it was raining really hard, and water was dripping off the tips of his boots that he had on, and I was directly under his boots. I kept clearing my eyes, because the water was dripping off his boots right into my eyes. I'm looking straight up at him, and all I could see are his fingers and his mouth – he's got his mouth hanging open and throwing his head back. I'm going, "This guy is *so* into it." I was 17 at the time and I was totally impressed. I ended up with mononucleosis – I shared a cigarette with somebody and they had mono, I guess. I was sick for a month.

KK DOWNING: Later, Jimi did the Isle of Wight [on August 31, 1970 (less than three weeks before his death)], and he was headlining – which was an open air music festival. I know, because I got fired from my job, because I left to go to that concert! And that was amazing, too. And I also went to see Jimi at the Royal Albert Hall [on February 24, 1969] – both of those shows – and got into the soundcheck, and got his autograph. I was in the press/photography pit at the Isle of Wight Festival, where he headlined. I was lucky enough to poke my head through their caravan, and get a drum stick and Jimi's Coca Cola bottle that he'd just finished drinking. I got lots of great memories.

And his impact in the States – he played Monterey and places like that, where he was just a powerhouse, and really into what he was doing. But, obviously, as time went on and he got involved in management, politics, the industry, things, some hardcore people, then he started to feel a bit dejected about, "Where is all this going? Everybody wants a piece of me." There is a lot of stuff on YouTube – the Isle of Wight show and the later stuff – you can see that Jimi was a bit affected. Which is very sad. And where he seemed to be going through the motions – where he wasn't in the beginning. It was just like he had the stuffing knocked out of him...or as some say, the shit kicked out of him, in some ways.

Obviously, his headspace was not in the same place he was in the first few years. His work rate got a bit wary, and I don't know what the situation was internally – with his bandmates. Were they wanting more of a piece of the pie? I understand it, because I've been through it myself. I can understand why bands go out there and literally go through the motions, and there are a lot of bands out there *now* that I get the same feeling from – ones that go through the motions. I guess a "free spirit" is what I was looking for – when Hendrix went out there, unaware of what the whole thing entailed.

ULI JON ROTH: I saw him live twice – the first time when he was at the peak of his musical zenith. That was the last Experience tour that he did in Europe – January '69, in Hamburg. And then I was at his very last show – the Isle of Fehmarn [on September 6, 1970], just a few days before he died.

I was lucky enough to be backstage, and I took a lot of photos. I didn't meet him – I was right next to him, but I didn't dare talk. He was obviously preoccupied with something and I was just 15 years old. I didn't want to "intrude." There were many people there. But I certainly will not forget that. And I was lucky to be at very close quarters during that show, and I took in the whole show. *I was right in front of him.**

*Quote is from the 2016 book, *German Metal Machine: Scorpions in the '70s*, by Greg Prato.

Chapter 3
Encounters

Memories of meeting or crossing paths with Jimi.

BUDDY GUY [singer/guitarist]: That was my first time ever playing in New York. I had just played Newport Jazz Fest, in 1967. I had never met him before. I was putting on my show, and I think I had the guitar behind my head – I had more energy than I've got now. And somebody kept whispering, *"There's Jimi Hendrix."* I saw this kid down on the floor, and they didn't have the little [recorders] like we've got now, where you can just press it. He had a reel-to-reel, and somebody was taping him with some kind of video. But when they said "Jimi Hendrix," I said, "Who in the hell is that?" He walked up to me and said, "I cancelled a concert to catch you, because I've been trying to catch you all my life. Can I tape what you're doing?" And I said, "I don't give a damn what you do."*

SCOTT GORHAM: I was 16 years old. My eventual brother-in-law, Bob Siebenberg from Supertramp, was with me, and we had another friend. Hendrix was playing up on the Earl Warren Showgrounds [on August 19, 1967]. He was the support act to Moby Grape. But we had no money to get into this concert. I had stolen my mom's car, and this friend of ours had taken his dad's World War II pistol, and he pawned it – for God sake's, what a

*Quote is from the *Rolling Stone* article, *Buddy Guy Sets the Record Straight With New Book*, by Greg Prato (April 25, 2012).

horrible thing that was – so we could have gas money. We finally get up there, and I'm questioning them the whole time, "How are we supposed to get in? We don't have any money!" And this guy says, "Don't say anything...*just follow me lead.*"

He had brought this old rusted tool chest with him, and I didn't ask any questions. We got there, we parked, he opened it up, and he gave me this lump of wire. He said, "Just put this around your shoulder." He pulled out this flashlight that didn't work, and then he took the tool chest himself, because he put his camera in there. He says, "We're going to go to the stage door. Don't anybody say anything...*just follow my lead.*"

So, knock on the door, and this big, fat, bearded security guy came out, and my friend says, "We're with the electric company." I thought, "*The electric company?* We're dead in the water now." But he says, "We got a call to do a job." The guy looks at us, looks out at the parking lot, and goes, "Alright...come on in." So, we walk in, and all I remember is this really dark corridor, and we had no idea where we were. The first trash can we found, we dumped all the stuff – the flashlight, the wire, and the case – but he took his camera out.

And I saw this lit doorway. We headed for that, rounded the corner, looked in...*and there was Hendrix* – leaning against the table, with his guitar, warming up. And my 16-year-old little brain just froze on the spot. I couldn't actually bring myself to say anything. And this buddy of mine comes breezing in, and says, "Hey Jimi, how ya doin'? Listen, do you mind if we take a coupla pictures?" And Hendrix goes, "Sure, no problem." He stood up, had his picture taken. We chatted for...it couldn't have been more than three minutes, and then he said, "Listen guys, hope you don't mind, but I have to warm up here." He shook everybody's hand, and said, "Listen, have a great time. I'll see you out front." And that was it, we were gone.

We made our way out to the auditorium, and we watched Hendrix – and he was amazing. And after he was done, three-quarters of the audience got up and left. So, Moby Grape just got the shit blown out of them – *a three-quarter empty hall*. I don't think I've ever seen anybody get so blown away in my life. Hendrix was really cool.

JACK CASADY [Jefferson Airplane bassist]: The memories are great [of playing bass on "Voodoo Chile," on May 2, 1968 at the Record Plant in NYC]. Jorma and I had been playing with Jefferson Airplane and I think we were doing *The Dick Cavett Show* taping earlier in the evening, and as we did back then, we always had our guitars with us. We finished up early and we went to go visit Steve Paul's the Scene in New York City, which was a small, half-underground club.

We wanted to hear a band that was coming over from England called Traffic. Our friends, Jimi Hendrix and Mitch Mitchell, came to the club to hear [Jimi's] buddies because he knew these guys. [Jimi] invited a bunch of us over to the studio and we listened to him record and hung out. It was a little different atmosphere than previous years because he had just started to produce his own work in the studio. With that kind of atmosphere, there was a lot more freedom in his approach.

In any case, we watched him overdub and work for a while and at about daybreak, he said, "Let's play a song." He showed us the chord changes to "Voodoo Chile" and we ran it over – I think a string broke. We did a full take and I think another full take, I can't remember. And Jorma and I had to leave because we had a gig in DC the next day, so we all piled into our LTD Station Wagons and drove down to Washington after the session at about 9am. It was a great time. He was a great guy to play with...Jimi was a very gracious man. He just looked you in the eye and you started to play. There were no hijinks, no nothing. He was a great musician and it was a lot of fun.*

DAVE MASON [Traffic singer/guitarist, solo artist]: Oh, God. What was I...19 years old, 20 years old? [When Mason was part of the *Electric Ladyland* sessions – contributing backing vocals and twelve-string guitar to "Crosstown Traffic" and "All Along the Watchtower"] It was just great. I mean, it was like, "Yeah, wow, this is cool." The way a lot of that happened was because it was the times and it was the place. In other words, we were in England, and the thing is, everybody finished up in London.

Everybody was using the studios in London, and there weren't many. There were only a few. And there were only a little handful of really good producers. So everybody was using the same studios, the same people. Like Jimmy Miller was brought

*Quote is from the *Long Island Pulse* article, *Hot Tuna Goes Electric For GSBMF*, by Greg Prato (June 27, 2018).

over to do Traffic and started doing the Stones. It was not unusual for people to drop by each other's sessions. The Beatles, that introduction came through a girl I was dating who was making some piece of furniture: a couch for Paul McCartney. It was a transparent couch with all the characters from the *Sgt. Pepper* album in it. So that's how I met McCartney. And through that, it was like, "Oh, you're Traffic? Oh, cool." That's how those things happened.

And Hendrix just happened to be sitting in one of those semi-private clubs in London. He was there one night just sitting alone, and it was like, "Fuck, I'm just going to go over and say 'Hi' and talk to him." So I started there, with that. He was a fan of Traffic, and I was lucky enough to actually get to do some things with him and play on one of his significant tracks, with a Bob Dylan song, "All Along the Watchtower." So, yeah. It was fun. It was cool.*

MICK BOX: The closest I got to him, at the Albert Hall, Joe Cocker was performing for the first time "With a Little Help from My Friends." And I think he had Badfinger supporting. I was in the queue, waiting to go into the Albert Hall to see this, and Jimi Hendrix was there – in full military outfit. He looked fantastic!

KK DOWNING: I got an autograph – I was waiting

*Quote is from the *Songfacts* article, *Songwriter Interviews: Dave Mason*, by Greg Prato (May 15, 2014).

outside the Royal Albert Hall, and I had a poster, and he signed it for me. Just Jimi. He had gone out to the car with a guitar – it was a white SG with three pickups. It was gold-plated. But I snuck into the soundcheck, so I saw that. But Jimi was in a...we call them caravans – I guess you call them a trailer – but I'm talking a '50s trailer. An antiquated kind of makeshift dressing room.

These things used to have windows all around the sides. The window wasn't closed, because it was quite warm, and me and my mate lifted the window up, and they had curtains, and we lifted the curtains aside, and we saw Jimi, Mitch was next to him, and there were two girls. So, cheeky cheeky me, I put my face in...and they told us to fuck off or something. [Laughs] I don't know if I asked them for the drum stick or the Coke bottle, but I got those items – and cherished them. But that was all it was really. So, that was my experience.

ACE FREHLEY [Kiss guitarist, solo artist]: The craziest thing happened to me. I was always a huge Hendrix fan, and Hendrix's last New York show was this big festival – right across the river from Manhattan is a place called Randall's Island [on July 17, 1970]. I couldn't have been more than 18 or 19 years old. I went to this festival, and I snuck backstage. In those days, they didn't have laminates and stick-on passes. I'm walking around with a black t-shirt with a snakeskin star on the front, lemon yellow hot pants, checkered Vans, and my hair is down to my waist!

I was watching the backstage entrance, and I just walked back there, and gave the security guy a nod – he thought I was in one of the bands! I was like a kid in a candy shop. But after about 15 minutes, somebody came up and said, *"Who are you?"* I said, "I'm just hanging out – I'm not really supposed to be here." They said, "Can you do anything?" I go, "Yeah, I can set up drums." So they put me on to work with the stage crew. The next thing I know, I'm setting up Mitch Mitchell's drum kit! I roadied for Jimi Hendrix, and got to shake his hand.*

*Quote is from an interview in *Guitarist*, by Greg Prato (2009).

Chapter 4
Classics

The crème de la crème.

KIRK HAMMETT: *Axis* is amazing in its own right, because of Jimi Hendrix's chordal style…all the various voicings that he fits in – all the diatonics, the little suspensions, the "happy accidents." That's what they sound like – things that he just *happened* on. It all starts on *Axis: Bold as Love.* And it starts with "Castles Made of Sand," "Little Wing," and "One Rainy Wish." He really started to develop that "Jimi Hendrix ballad style." When you *really* look at that format, it's based on an R&B structure. Almost all music has a formula – all styles have certain formulas behind it. And if you play enough styles of music, you can get pretty familiar with these formulas.

Over the years, I've become familiar with a lot of formulas in jazz, blues, country, rock, folk, gypsy jazz, soul, and R&B. Even heavy metal has its formulas. But a lot of those ballads – particularly "Castles Made of Sand," "Little Wing," and "One Rainy Wish" – are so "R&B chord formula." But the great thing is he takes that structure and opens it up harmonically so much more, so it becomes so much more lyrical. And opens up so many more voicings and suspensions. That in itself is just pretty miraculous.

The person who innovated that whole type of approach was Curtis Mayfield. And Curtis Mayfield was just trying to play certain parts of the chords to embellish his vocals. So, he would figure out what parts of the chords mattered the most and just played those notes. And he developed a completely lyrical chord style that Jimi took and just ran with. He made it something completely different and over the top – as far as lyrical beauty is concerned. And he made it *his own thing*. For me, that is such a huge influence, too.

What Jimi does is he dresses up all the chords and positions, and what I choose to do is if I write a progression, I'll just dress up one of those chords in the progression the way Jimi Hendrix might. It adds a lot more form and uniqueness to the progression. It's just a great thing.

STEVE VAI: *Axis: Bold as Love* was the Jimi record that I discovered when I was learning my chord vocabulary on the guitar. Because when you go to learn chords on the guitar, you usually get a list of tablature chords and you use your open chords, your major and minor barre chords, maybe you're learning some cool seventh chords, or major-minor chords, and chords from tensions. I was really big on finding chords that sounded really *lush*. I remember when I discovered an E flat major seventh six nine sharp eleventh chord – it opened up a universe for me. And I knew why it was called all that – I had great musical training.

But what I didn't have was the ability to make sense...I mean, I knew how chord progressions are conventionally put together on diatonic strings, but making my chord playing actually sound like music was alien to me. At best, I could learn a jazz chord solo standard. But it was very conventional. But, when I started listening deeply to Jimi's chord playing, that was an epiphany. It was exactly everything that I loved about playing chords on the guitar. And the *Axis* record, you can *really* hear it. If you listen to his chord playing on those songs...and "Little Wing" is an obvious example – that whole intro. Eddie Kramer gave me a tape of various takes of "Little Wing" – I think it's available now – and every one of them is wildly different. And every one of them is completely inspired in the moment. That's stunning to me.

I'm going to be 60 this year – Hendrix was 27 when he died. He slipped in from the abyss and presented a monolith. He was a monolith at raising the bar. And that record...I learned every song as close as I could to the way he was playing it. And it's miraculously beautiful how he does his chording. If you listen to songs like "Castles Made of Sand" – any of that stuff on that record and any of his other records when you can really hear him "chording" around, it's just magnificent.

And it doesn't follow any standard. It's not confined to a particular genre. So, there was a period of time there, where that was the basis of my entire chordal playing vocabulary. And then obviously, I picked up other things from other people and incorporated it into my playing. But I think I may have said that I had a special connection with *Axis*. It really was my mentor.

RICHARD LLOYD: I think his apex was the second album, *Axis: Bold as Love*. I *love* that record. That's a great record. A lot of his more intricate solos were on *Electric Ladyland* – which is also a fantastic record. I remember being confused by it a bit when I first heard it – it's pretty sprawling. But it's got "House Burning Down" and phenomenal guitar stuff on it. Of course, everybody is going to mention "Voodoo Child (Slight Return)" – which didn't really speak to me as much as some of the straighter songs that Chas [Chandler] had to do with.

ADRIAN BELEW: In particular, I really love the first three records – *Are You Experienced, Axis: Bold as Love,* and *Electric Ladyland.* There's enough guitar information in those three records to fill an encyclopedia. I studied Jimi Hendrix deep into my career. Even after I had figured out how to do many of his trademarks, I have always continued to reference him.

Favorite songs and standout moments: I've already mentioned the outer space sound of "Purple Haze," next there's the brute force fuzz guitar complimenting Mitch's ricochet drumming on "Manic Depression." Other favorites from *Are You Experienced* include "May This Be Love," where Jimi emulates the sounds of a waterfall with tape delay, the amazing controlled feedback intro to "Fire," "Third Stone from the Sun's" trippy use of tape modulation, and my favorite, second only to "Purple Haze" – the title track from *Are You Experienced*, with it's incredible reverse tape backwards guitar solo, the one that changed my playing forever.

Axis: Bold as Love opens with his spaceman persona front and center with "EXP," and "Up from the Skies," which features some of the his most soulful wah wah playing ever, and a kind of "cool jazz" rhythm section from Mitch and Noel. Mitch's drumming on the entire record is stunning. Other favorite tracks include "You Got Me Floatin'" and "Castles Made of Sand," both featuring backwards guitar, "If 6 Was 9's" powerful vocal attitude, and two masterpiece Hendrix creations – "Little Wing" (beautiful rhythm playing and dreamy vocal effects) and "Axis: Bold As Love," with its massive stereo flanging drum fill leading into the majestic searing guitar reprise. There are so many innovative guitar sounds on this one record – as well as some of his best songwriting and lyrics.

I have three particular favorites from *Electric Ladyland* – "1983 (A Merman I Should Turn to Be)" has a beautiful opening guitar line and more gorgeous backwards guitar (man, I'm a sucker for backwards guitar!), "House Burning Down," and yet another masterpiece, "All Along the Watchtower." His guitar playing in "Watchtower" impresses me most, because it's basically clean guitar sounds, a little slide guitar playing and some wah wah, but no explosive distortion he so often favored. As far as a hit single featuring great guitar playing, it doesn't get any better in my opinion.

ULI JON ROTH: My all-time favorite stuff used to be on *Axis: Bold as Love*. In fact, the title track itself is my favorite Hendrix solo. But then, you have the other side of Hendrix, like, doing the "Machine Gun" solo – from *Band of Gypsys*. That is a totally different level of playing, a totally different way of playing – not as melodic, but just as totally descriptive. So, these two extremes. I also loved *Electric Ladyland*...but maybe not every song. But certainly, the highlights – from "Watchtower" to "House

Burning Down," and "Gypsy Eyes." Unbelievable stuff he came up with – in a short four years. It was just an unbelievable burst of energy. *Creative energy.*

No two Hendrix songs were ever the same – they were all in his own style, which was very, very unique. But, they also really had their own individual "face" and identity. There is no song in the world like "Purple Haze," there is no other song like "Little Wing," there is no other song like "Axis," there is no other song like "House Burning Down" or "Gypsy Eyes" or "Hey Joe." They're all completely unique. And many artists are not able to do that kind of thing – they find a formula, and they repeat it over and over again, kind of. I think that was extraordinary – what Hendrix did. And the list goes on...literally, *anything* – "Burning of the Midnight Lamp," "The Wind Cries Mary" and the early stuff, "Third Stone from the Sun," you name it.

ALEX LIFESON: "Manic Depression." The solo is totally...*manic!* "Are You Experienced" – I'd never heard anything like it. I've done my share of backward recording, but the solo is perfect in that song. "All Along the Watchtower." Gorgeous production, best acoustic guitar sound, and the solo is sublime. The "slide half" is dreamy and dripping with feel, and the "wah wah half" is such a cool melody and execution – not to mention the sweeping pumping mix effect. Keep in mind, the wah wah had just come on the scene and was one of the only few effects – including the Fuzz Face – available.

SCOTT GORHAM: "The Wind Cries Mary" is all

these chordal/lead-y kind of things he does, rather than flat-out single note kind of things. It was the first time I ever heard a guitar player use a chordal kind of system as a lead break. And I just thought that was *so* cool. I still try to emulate it today – those kind of chordal little lead things. It really struck me in a big way.

KK DOWNING: When you're such an avid fan like me – and really, the content was not overly in abundance at the time of his death – I think everything he did was just *magical*. The things that do stick out in my mind, that was the first time I ever heard heavy metal in my life. The first time I heard songs like "Foxy Lady" and "Purple Haze," the song structures determine that they're not a blues song – but a *progressive* blues song. There's something different. And a lot of stuff he would do that was kind of imaginative and full of escapism – "1983." All of that kind of stuff was in a different genre, to my ears.

I was an aspiring musician, and I think the only song of Jimi's that I ever played live was "Spanish Castle Magic" – only because we didn't have enough originals to put a setlist together. But I never wanted to copy Hendrix. I never wanted to be a soundalike or anything like that. I just think consciously or subconsciously, I took everything onboard, and just wanted to create something different, and a style like he created for himself, and other bands had created for themselves – whether it was Zeppelin, Sabbath, or other bands.

What I was doing, I knew to be successful, you had to be original, and you couldn't step on stage and people go, "Ah-ha! I know where these chaps are coming from." That didn't work. I was smart enough not to just try and draw from other individuals as I went along.

RIK EMMETT: No doubt about it, "Watchtower" is to me the pinnacle of how good it possibly gets. It was a pretty good song...from a pretty good songwriter! And Jimi had an irreverent kind of approach to Dylan – he loved him. But the song and the production of it, and the guitar solos themselves – further to my point that I made earlier, some of those solos are *rhythm solos* [sings part of "Watchtower" solo].

That's just so "rhythmically pure" – such a great, great idea. And who'd ever done that before? *No one.* So, the guitar tones that are in that – just everything. He clearly had an ability to visualize what it was that he was trying to do, so he had a really clear picture in his mind of what he was trying to create – in terms of sound, note selection, and all that stuff. That's as good as it gets – as far as that's concerned.

BRUCE KULICK: Who doesn't go, "Wow!" when you hear "All Along the Watchtower"? He uses effects and plays such emotional leads. But then there are tracks like, "If 6 Was 9," when he got *really* crazy. Just all the backwards guitars and that title track from *Are You Experienced*. I don't think there is a track that I can go "snooze" to. *This guy owned it.* He connected to the instrument in a way that was totally magical. It became an expression of his inner-voice – between the feedback, the overtones, and how he can control his instrument.

And with a Stratocaster being really a wild beast – single coil pickups – they're very varied in the brightness to the darkness. But he was just able to make so many different sonic tones come out of it, that were so emotional, that it's always been one of my biggest inspirations as a lead guitarist. From "Purple Haze" to "Foxy Lady." "Machine Gun" is considered one of those epic moments for Hendrix to set the stage for an experience of being in the jungles of the Vietnam War. It's really an incredible feat.

His solos were just *so* filled with expression. I love the Beatles when they got experimental, so one side that I wore out – totally – when I got the vinyl, was *Electric Ladyland*, and that whole side with "1983 (A Merman I Should Turn to Be)." It was like he was on the acid trip and you listening to him...*you're there with him.*

RON "BUMBLEFOOT" THAL: "Fire," "Crosstown Traffic," I always liked "Manic Depression" – I just like things that are in three and swing. "Little Wing," of course. "Castles," "If 6 Was 9" – I loved the space in it, and then when the space closes.

DOUG PINNICK: The first two records continually blow my mind, because nobody did that before. The way he wrote songs..."I Don't Live Today" – it's a verse, a chorus, and a jam, and a chorus and extends. Or "If 6 Was 9" – it's two verses, a middle part, and this long jam out. And it sounded like he was just throwing it off the cuff, because sometimes, the musicians picked up on it – he'd be changing keys and doing something else, and they're *still* on the other riff!

The recklessness of the way he wrote is in his music, and the genius of it just worked so well. I know a lot of people think he was a hack and didn't play well, but how are you going to play well when you're going for something you never went for before? That's the whole point – *he went for things*, and he wasn't afraid to crawl to it in public. It seems like a lot of live stuff I've heard him do, they say he didn't play well. But it didn't matter – he was still Jimi.

MICK MARS [Mötley Crüe guitarist]: Probably my favorite [is *Axis: Bold as Love*]. I think that's when Jimi started becoming a real songwriter. By the time of his *Are You Experienced* album he was getting the feel of it, although maybe he was still a little embarrassed about his singing. Hearing his stuff on *Axis* was him going to another level of his talent. His playing and writing was getting better. By the time they reached *Electric Ladyland,* with all that jamming and craziness that was going on, it was way over the top.*

BILLY SHEEHAN: I remember putting on *Band of Gypsys*, and my next door neighbor had a turntable, too – so he brought it over and we plugged it into my amp, and then played my regular record player. We both had a copy of it, so we tried to play it so that they would both sync up. It would start to

*Quote is from the *Classic Rock* article, *Mötley Crüe's Mick Mars: The 10 Records That Changed My Life*, by Greg Prato (June 6, 2017).

get a little out of sync and get echoey and would sound like we were in a huge auditorium. We would drive the neighbors crazy with that! We just listened to it over and over and over again. And I listened to every little detail of the *Electric Ladyland* album – to this day there isn't a note, a sound, a click, or a pop that I don't remember off those records. It just became such a building block for me and my mind and music.

RANDY HANSEN: "Machine Gun" – absolutely. Because it's so long. And that one long note that he holds in there [at the 4:00 mark] – he was right in the eye of the storm, right there. He had a set-up on stage at that point to be able to do certain things. And he knew he was recording that night, so I'm sure that he did a really thorough soundcheck. They were there for a day ahead of time soundchecking and getting things to work. And it has to do with the right volume, standing in the right places – you can hear it.

I go for that note every time *we* play "Machine Gun," and probably one time out of a hundred, it will stay. Jimi, it stayed for him that night. Maybe we should do better soundchecks or something – I don't know. But that one is a bitch. I'm dealing with different things though – I don't have Jimi's Marshalls and I don't have Jimi's guitar and I don't have Jimi's pedals and Jimi's everything. Maybe all the magic is in there. Because I feel I've never totally ever captured it…and probably never will. But it makes a fun venture, anyway. His live performance of "Johnny B. Goode" I'd say was definitely like, "*Whoa!*" And then of course, "Wild

Thing."

But there is so much live stuff that you can see now. I even like the ones where Jimi's not happy, and you're going, "This is great...*but he's not happy*!" The day that I saw him he wasn't happy. He got really pissed off that day – they threw a big fluorescent pink pillow and a magic marker up to him, and he booted the pillow off the stage. And then he went to the microphone, and said, "Can you please not throw anything up on the stage, because I was over a friend's house last night, and I got kinda stoned on some scotch...and I feel like jumping on some cat's head, anyway."

He was mad at somebody, and was not in a good mood to play – and it was raining. But still, even after all that, his release was the guitar, so every time he got into the song, he'd get into that, instead. And you couldn't tell he was in a bad mood anymore – but when he stopped playing, he was. I'd never seen nothing like that before or since.

KIRK HAMMETT: My favorite Jimi Hendrix solo is really easy, because the song is *one giant fuckin' guitar solo with lyrics* – "Machine Gun." The original version on *Band of Gypsys*. It is *so* haunting and atmospheric. But he stays in that same kind of vein, and that same feel throughout. He was able to maintain that feel for what...ten minutes or something? And to just stay in that vein and that mood, and to sustain it – without it getting tired or tedious or boring – man, that's an accomplishment.

And he plays his ass off. He's bending notes, he's playing melodically, and then he's playing in a blues way, and then he hits these really outrageous singing/crying notes. It's so atmospheric and every note is so appropriate and in the right place. It's just amazing. But my favorite track these days on that album is "Power of Soul" – because it sounds like prog rock. It progresses through all these different riffs and progressions, and it makes its way back around. I love it. Jimi's playing is *so great* on that track.

BRIAN TATLER: My favorite Hendrix song – by a mile – is "Voodoo Child." I just think it's one of the greatest rock performances of all-time. I still listen to it from time to time now, and it's just incredible. It's probably one take...there might have been multiple takes, but picked one. And it's just *brimming* with ideas. You can hear him move the pickup selector and switch the wah wah on and off, and hold notes until they feedback. Ringing notes out of the neck. It's just an amazing performance – I can only imagine putting something down on tape that exciting and powerful.

There's a video performance of him from Blackpool, that just appeared on *The Old Grey Whistle Test* one night, and I had a video recorder and taped it. I think he did two songs. Just the way he held the guitar and moved around, it felt like part of him. It felt natural. Just amazing to watch – I'm fascinated by the way he plays the guitar and makes it look easy. Because any guitarist that has been playing for a while will tell you, it's *not* easy. I've been playing over 40 years now, and I can't do what Hendrix did! Incredible talent.

REVEREND HORTON HEAT: "Little Wing" is

a work of art. He did vintage stuff, too – he did "Johnny B. Goode." That was cool. His take on the modern stuff, like "All Along the Watchtower," the guitar parts on that song are *epic*. Woodstock is the main thing I would have liked to have seen of Jimi Hendrix.

CURT KIRKWOOD: I love "Little Wing," "The Wind Cries Mary"...I'm not good with titles sometimes!

PAUL LEARY: I was into the first album up through *Cry of Love*. Each one I kind of associate with a different phase of my life. "The Wind Cries Mary" because it was fun to play, the song "Are You Experienced" – the guitar was just non-stop expression, it was so far beyond the rhythm instrument. The same with "Fire." That aspect of his music is what stands out to me. And he had a drummer that was kind of the same way.

CHEETAH CHROME: I'm kind of partial to "Little Wing." And the whole first album is great. "Fire" and "Manic Depression" definitely had a punk vibe to it. And the one with the backwards guitar – "Are You Experienced."

EAST BAY RAY: I like "Fire," "Foxy Lady," "Purple Haze, "All Along the Watchtower," "Voodoo Child." Nowadays, I have things on an iPod, so I listen to a shuffle. But I also like Jimi's *Blues* record. "If Six Was Nine" and "Little Wing" off *Axis: Bold as Love*, "May This Be Love."

KIM THAYIL: The first albums I got I believe were *Cry of Love* and *Are You Experienced*. Those were the two albums I had for *years* – probably a decade or more. I might have acquired them from Bruce Pavitt – Sub Pop Records' co-founder – via trades. I probably gave up something like Santana's *Greatest Hits* or a Be-Bop Deluxe album. But I loved the Hendrix records. So I became very familiar with the material on *Cry of Love* – which is very sophisticated and technical, and as a young kid, I thought, "Wow…that's impressive!"

Songs like "Freedom" and "Ezy Ryder" are really cool. But the whole album was cool – different tones and emotional things, like "Belly Button Window," "My Friend." *Are You Experienced* is more of a…every song is hooky and strong and to the point. It's a rock classic. I think definitely more emotive and artistic things are perhaps explored on *Cry of Love*, but then again, that was a posthumous album, so sometimes people see that as non-canonical. I think of it as being part of it – it's him singing, he wrote the songs.

CASPAR BRÖTZMANN: I love him no matter what he is playing. I love him for all of his wonderful music, his trying to get and find some freedom, and that he had this time on earth to show the world his big talent to play loud electric guitar, Marshall amps and his spirit and thoughts he wrote down in his song lyrics, letters, and so on. I am ever thankful for "The Blue Wild Angel." You are asking me to elevate some moments of his playing, here are my favorites – I would like to distinguish his songs playing as live versions and as studio versions.

Of course, I love the studio versions of "Voodoo Child (Slight Return)" and "All Along the Watchtower," "Are You Experienced," and a few other songs. But I love how he is playing his music live on stage. Many years he was my master and secret companion, and many years ago he let me go and I turned off – going my way. My favorite records of Jimi Hendrix are *Isle of Wight Festival*, *Woodstock*, *Band of Gypsys*, *Live at Berkeley* ("Johnny B. Goode," "Purple Haze," and "Hear My Train A Comin'"), and *War Heroes*.

My absolute favorite record and film of Jimi Hendrix is the *Isle of Wight Festival.* He played on his absolute best high level a few days before he died. The live version of "Foxy Lady" at this festival is for me absolutely great and was inspiring to me, also how he played "All Along the Watchtower." *Woodstock*, *Live at Berkeley*, and the song "Machine Gun" live with the Band of Gypsys are also my very favorites in film and music.

BRUCE KULICK: All the records, the common thread is Jimi's guitar playing, the unique style that he has. I think he was evolving as an artist – and you hear that. But if I made a playlist of Hendrix from *Axis* and the first album, those two albums are not that radically different [from each other]. I think he got even more comfortable in the studio on the second record. But for that first record, what he was doing? *Unbelievable.* And again, that was his first effort and he probably had a single or two first. He was already putting his stamp on what kind of artist he was.

And then certainly *Electric Ladyland* being a

double album, but none of it was recorded at Electric Lady Studios – which is kind of tragic. He spread out a lot more on that one – that one is a bit more evolved, just like the way *Sgt. Pepper* compared to *Beatles for Sale* or *A Hard Day's Night*. You see the evolution. Now, the live record, *Band of Gypsys* – which is technically the fourth one released – that's a whole other animal. He's experimenting with different people. And you know that by late '69 into '70, he was very despondent with being "a hero" maybe, or a star. I think business-wise, he was being overworked – a lot of pressure on him, that I can only imagine was crushing him, sadly.

KIRK HAMMETT: The song "Angel" is one of my most favorite Jimi Hendrix songs, as well. I named my first son after that song. My son's name is Angel Ray – "Angel" is from that song and "Ray" is from Stevie Ray Vaughan. I also love that Jimi Hendrix loved Hawaii. And the song "Pali Gap" – Pali is a range of mountains that splits Oahu's south side and east side. That's what that song is about.

And there's footage of Jimi all over Bali and Oahu in *Rainbow Bridge*. Also, you know what's great about *Rainbow Bridge*? The surf footage! The surf footage in *Rainbow Bridge* is really great, because those guys are actually really bonafide Hawaiian pro surfers from the '70s that would compete. So, that footage is really important archival footage of '70s surfing – *just for the record.*

Chapter 5
Steve & Joe Bond Over Jimi

When Steve Vai was a young guitar student being taught by Joe Satriani on Long Island, New York, Jimi's music provided inspiration for both.

STEVE VAI: Absolutely, unequivocally – Joe introduced me towards the depths of Hendrix, because he could actually play the songs and he would show me the songs. Being able to play and put your hands on a guitar and have something that sounds like the song that your hero is playing come out of it was addictive. It was a surprise and a delight. And that was why I started playing.

It was two reasons – that and the other reason was having my own ideas and then working on the instrument until they came out. That made every day like Christmas, y'know? There was nothing else as remotely interesting to me as that. I don't believe my story is a unique one – it's very common from so many guitar players that Jimi helped shape their playing or even kicked it off.

First, there was "The Star-Spangled Banner" [that Joe taught Steve] – because that was all I listened to. And oddly enough, for some years after that, I started to decide that, "I am going to see this guy play. I *have to* see him play." I didn't even realize he had died – until I was twelve or thirteen. As far as my views, the standout Hendrix tracks have always been "Voodoo Child" – just because of the aggression. Songs like "Midnight." And penultimate is probably "Machine Gun" – that's about as close as you're going to get to the voice of God on a guitar.

The connection.

My older brother, Roger, was actually at that concert – it was New Year's Eve. Satriani told me a great story because Bill Graham was the promoter of that show, and Bill was Joe's manager at one point. I hope I get the story correct, but Bill was very supportive and hands-on, and he would observe shows and then kind of give critiques for the improvement of them. It was two shows that night, and after the first show, supposedly Jimi was out there doing his whole thing – throwing the guitar around and playing with his teeth.

And after the show, he said to Bill, "What did you think of the show?" And Bill said, "Well, you're obviously an incredible guitar player...but I don't think you need to do all these antics. They're not really necessary for your musicianship." Or something along those lines. So, like most artists who are tremendously sensitive about these kinds of critiques, it's not uncommon that they take it personally. Seeing that, perhaps, Hendrix took it a particular way, and when he went out to do a second show, he just stood there and didn't move a muscle – *for the entire show.* And that's where the performance of "Machine Gun" came from. And then for the last encore...he came out and *destroyed* the stage.

Those are standouts, but then there are the beautifully experimental production pieces – like "Are You Experienced." That song – in and of itself – is just legions above what others were trying to capture at that time. At least for me. It encompassed the psychedelia at a tolerable level – even an infectious level. And it also had great guitar skills and incredibly beautiful songwriting. The lyrics are to die for. And the experimentation – backwards guitars sounding as perfectly in place as anything ever recorded. That's how that song fell into my ears.

And then, there were songs like "1983 (A Merman I Should Turn To Be)" on *Electric Ladyland*. For some reason, that song *really* captured me – along with "Rainy Day, Dream Away," which more than any other Hendrix song, feels to me that it captured an atmosphere, besides the music. The song "Midnight" is *so* beautiful. It's like a tour de force of thrash freedom on the guitar.

Chapter 6
Influence Covers Disciples

Tracing Jimi's influence on other guitarists, memories of covering his music, and those who are considered "Jimi disciples."

RANDY HANSEN: I was in a comedy band called Kid Chrysler and the Cruisers. I'd been in the band for less than a year, and we were out on our night off, and we saw this comedy duo do a fictitious character that was a little bit like Alice Cooper, and he crawled up the mic stand like a snake, and flung his tongue out – his tongue thing reminded me of Jimi right away. And then Henry [the band's bassist] leans over to me, and goes, "We need to add another show. We need to make fun of rock stars. Who would you want to make fun of?" And I said, "Well, I wouldn't want to 'make fun of him'…but I want to do Jimi Hendrix if you're going to do that." He said, "OK, *do that.*"

And I swear to God that was the first rock tribute band – because that was in 1975, and that's when I started to do the tribute to Jimi Hendrix. And that's what I called it right away – "Randy Hansen's Machine Gun: A Tribute to Jimi Hendrix." I got kicked out of that band by Kid Chrysler, who pointed out that the agency was ready to book me as this Hendrix tribute. So, I just came out with that Randy Hansen's Machine Gun: A Tribute to Jimi Hendrix. And it was such a unique thing – there was nothing like that out there. I had the whole field to myself at that time – which was kind of wonderful. [Laughs]

What ended up happening is Heart came to see me, and they put me on tour with them – which I got kicked off of their tour after two shows! But they passed me off to the Beach Boys and the Kinks. And then *they* passed me off. I never did more than one or two shows with these bands. And I put it down as, "This is the power of Jimi Hendrix's music" – because the crowds were going nuts. They probably thought they were never going to hear a Jimi Hendrix song like this played live again…or a whole bunch of them.

I was so jazzed about doing it back then that people told me that I looked like I was on speed up there. Probably my heart was pumping that fast, anyway – I went from playing little clubs to immediately playing in front of 10,000 people. It was shocking to me. And then to go around the country like this with these other huge bands…and then we eventually played at the Day on the Green [in 1980], in front of 75,000 people!

I was just going, "Man…*how did we get here*?" Someone asked me when I first started doing it, "What do you think this is going to lead to?" And I said, "I have no idea. But we're going to find out." And that's the approach I've taken ever since – I want to see where this is going to lead to. And it's led to me being an old man – I'm 65 years old now, and I'm still playing it and people are still turning out in droves to see me. I love it. I couldn't have spent my life in a better way. I always tell people, "I've got the best job in the world."

FRANK MARINO: When I started – before I had albums – going back to the days of '69, 'cause I started playing in '68. So, going into '69, and then '70, and then Hendrix dies, and then by '71 I record an album [1972's *Maxoom*]. I'm a kid – I'm 16 years old going on 17 when I record it. Prior to that, getting ready to do the album...what was I going to cover before doing albums? I was going to cover music of the day. That's what bands did – they went and played a high school gym or outside in the park, because in those days, you could do that...you'd just bring a generator and start playing. It's just what we did.

So, what are you going to play? You haven't written a lot of songs. You're 16 years old. You're going to cover whatever tunes are cool. So, what's cool for a guitar? At the time, Jimi Hendrix is pretty cool. Johnny Winter is pretty cool. Santana is pretty cool. *For a guitar*. But you're only going to cover tunes that are really guitar-based, like something from *Sgt. Pepper* or even something from the Stones, or Deep Purple doing "Hush" – before they became the "Deep Purple" that we all know. So, that was perfectly normal. But, because you're playing three-piece music, you're more likely to cover Jimi Hendrix tunes or Cream tunes. So, that's what we did.

I got to the point where I could play pretty much any Jimi Hendrix tune – it was easy for me, because it was my natural style. I didn't have to think about how to do it – I just naturally played that way. It was like, "That's the easiest thing to do, so I'm going to do that." You name a Jimi Hendrix tune, and there wasn't a tune I never played. At some point, I played every one of them – from all of his albums. That's fine, but when you then go into recording life, you're not just going to cover every Jimi Hendrix tune, so, you're going to pick the ones that you think,

"These would be pretty cool to cover." Then, when people start covering them, I'd rather cover a different one.

The "Watchtower" thing is a totally different animal. You have to understand, by the time I did "All Along the Watchtower" [on 1979's *Tales of the Unexpected*], I was having that giant war with the press over Jimi Hendrix – to put that in context. I said to myself, "Hey, I'm going to cover 'All Along the Watchtower' in the style that Hendrix did it. And when they scream about it, I'm going to tell them it's a Bob Dylan tune." That basically was my reason for doing that tune. And I did. And that's exactly what happened.

Because there are people out there who thought it was a Jimi Hendrix tune. We know it's a Bob Dylan tune done by Hendrix, but a lot of those writers didn't. Which sort of exposes their ignorance of the music they cover. It was a snub back at you. But on the same record, I covered a Beatles tune – "Norwegian Wood." Nobody mentions *that one* though. [Laughs]

The interesting thing about what I do on a record is if you actually go look at those records from those days is one of the main complaints that the record companies always had with me – whether it was 20th Century or Columbia – was, "Why are you doing so many different styles on an album?" They wanted me to play one thing. They said, "Successful bands play one thing. AC/DC is AC/DC on every song." But my records have a funk tune, and a jazz tune, and a blues tune, and a ballad, and a psychedelic tune. All the records follow that pattern.

But most people don't know – they'll hear

"Dragonfly" because that's the one the radio played, or they might hear "Strange Dreams." But they're not going to go back and look at these albums and find out that there were songs like "Lady," "Hey Little Lover," and all these other ones. To them, they're "secondary tunes." But when they're in front of you, you go, "Hey, this is a funk tune, this is a jazz tune, this song's in 5/4." That's because of my roots as a drummer. Everything I do when I play music, I happen to be playing guitar because guitar is what was in the hospital [explained in the next chapter]. Had it been drums, I would have stuck with drums. But I still approach music as a drummer and I write most of my tunes as a drummer, and consequently, the drummers in my band can play a lot of stuff – they're very free. So, that's probably why there is a funk element in songs like "Dragonfly."

KIRK HAMMETT: The second guitar solo that I learned how to play – that I felt that I was getting really close and actually learning something from it – was "The Wind Cries Mary." Again, that was almost unusual, because he's taking the "Curtis Mayfield lyrical chordal style" and he's interjecting it into a guitar solo, which is again, just amazing. It's basically the same idea, but he's picking out parts of these chords and highlighting everything in the guitar solo section. And it taught me how to be melodic and lyrical and to really put respect on a chordal approach. So, the guitar solo in "The Wind Cries Mary" was *really* important for me.

To this day, Jimi Hendrix and Michael Schenker were basically my main influences. Bar none. And because Jimi Hendrix was a blues player,

I wanted to learn the blues – and I started listening to BB King, Muddy Waters, Buddy Guy, Howlin' Wolf...*all* those guys. And just learning about all these guys through Jimi. Like, "Catfish Blues" is Muddy Waters. Jimi was always talking about blues artists, and I would always take little mental notes. And my other three favorite guitar players – Eric Clapton because I was a big Cream fan, Jimmy Page because I was a big Zeppelin fan, and Jeff Beck because Beck was just *so* fuckin' badass – were blues-based also, which made me totally want to learn the blues. Which I did.

I've come to the realization now – 40 years into my guitar playing life – that my whole style has a blues foundation. And I like that fact, because it kind of sets me apart from a lot of my peers – whose foundation may be more rock-based or commercially-influenced. I can solidly say that if you tear away all the layers, I'm a blues player at the very core of my playing. So, I like the blues feel, the blues phrasing – it feels so natural. And all my favorite players played those pentatonic scales, as well. So, that's how much of an influence Jimi was for me in the beginning.

JOE SATRIANI [Chickenfoot guitarist, solo artist]: Oh, so much. [In response to the question, "How much of an influence would you say Jimi Hendrix is still on your playing?"]. The thing that I really constantly remember from Jimi's playing was he had a way of being different song to song. He just would not hit you over the head with this same guitar sound, over and over again. He would have something different. And then his playing would be different.

Like on one song, he could play fast and fluid, and then on the next, it sounded like he was struggling to play slow. And one song, his guitar would be spacey, and the other song it would be clear and played right in your face with nothing special added to it. And I loved that. Just being a fan of putting on a record and listening to it all the way through, by the time you got to the end, you'd go, "Wow. I've got to hear that again. That had so many different sides to it." And what you were really hearing was all the different sides of his musicianship.

I constantly remind myself that it's OK in this day and age where people really do like to homogenize and compact and promote one idea and hit you over the head with it, Jimi's era really allowed for him to be much more creative with a guitar. And I'm using "the same one" - I've got the same six strings on it, and there's no reason to do the same thing over and over again.

This record [2015's *Shockwave Supernova*] certainly bears witness to the fact that I was influenced by his creativity and creating many different guitar sounds, and that's what we did with this record: We allowed so many different guitar sounds to be the hallmark of each song. We didn't worry about trying to promote "Joe Satriani the guitar player." It's really about the music.*

*Quote is from the *Songfacts* article, *Songwriter Interviews: Joe Satriani*, by Greg Prato (June 19, 2015).

BILLY SHEEHAN: For me, I got influenced by a lot of musicians on a lot of instruments. Eddie Harris on sax, John Coltrane on sax, Arthur Peterson on piano – a lot of different instruments. Bach's "Cello Suites" – you name it. So, it wasn't always about just bass and bass only, and only approved bass tones on approved basses by approved bass players. Some room to move out of that box a little bit. So, I heard Tim Bogert play, and he played with distortion. And I heard Jack Bruce play, and he played with distortion, too. It became a thing early on for me – to want to turn my amp up, to distort it and take it from there.

So, Jimi became a part of it because he – like all players – decided to do more with his instrument. On bass, why not do more? Why not get something feeding back? Why not hold a note? Why not have a little screaming distortion? Jimi basically took the whole rulebook and threw it out – it was great for everybody. Though abiding by those rules is important and good, it's good to know that nobody is holding a gun to your head to do that anymore – you can start to move. And that worked for drummers, singers, songwriters, and of course, bass players. That's the spirit that the Hendrix thing was.

At the time, I was into some great bass players - Paul Samwell-Smith from the Yardbirds was all over the place and was fantastic. James Jamerson from Motown – I loved that stuff and he was all over the place. Paul McCartney – all over the place. Jimi Hendrix was Jimi Hendrix, Mitch Mitchell was a mind-blowing drummer, but I thought Noel Redding was…even at that early age before I had the ability to be critical of anything – because I didn't know anything – in the back of my mind, I'm going, "*This* is the best they've got for Jimi? I don't know, man." I hate to be critical of any other musician, but I just thought, "Man, what a golden opportunity to do more. Not to get in Jimi's way – but to build a better framework around him."

I still love all those songs and I love all the bass parts, so it's not like he blew it by any means. But then when Billy Cox played, I loved that he was so locked in with Buddy Miles. It just sounded so beefier, monstrous, and giant that it really opened up a lot more room for Jimi to play. And then Jack Casady played some stuff on *Electric Ladyland*, which I thought was so great – a couple of bass solo thingies and moves that he did that were fantastic. Because he had a cool and unique tone – I love Jack Casady, he's one of my favorite players, ever. And having him in there I thought was a cool thing.

I was a little bit disappointed with Noel Redding early on. It wasn't until later on that I look back and go, "Y'know, he could have done this a little differently." But I'm sure there are people that will say, "If he would have, it would be too much and it wouldn't have worked and it might have sucked." It could very well be. Once it's put onto vinyl, you never know what could have been or how it would have gone down. It might not have been good at all.

SCOTT GORHAM: Completely. [In response to being asked, "Was Phil Lynott a fan of Jimi?"] He idolized Hendrix – he just thought he was the greatest guitar player to ever walk the planet. Phil loved everything about him – the way he looked, the way he dressed, the way he played, the way he moved on stage. *The whole thing.* And I think Phil probably stole a few bits from Hendrix – the stage presence side and all that. If you're going to emulate somebody, that's not a bad role model to go with!

KIM THAYIL: Chris [Cornell] and I had been in this other band before Soundgarden – a cover band. And not a very good cover band. I was playing bass and Chris was singing…and that band also did some Doors and Otis Redding. And we did the song "Can You See Me" by Hendrix.

So, I believe Soundgarden were in England and we were going to record some songs for a BBC session [in 1992], and that was the session where we did "I Don't Care About You" by Fear, "I Can't Give You Anything" by the Ramones, and "Homicidal Suicidal" by Budgie. And those radio guys were interested in a fourth song, so I said to Chris, "Why don't we do 'Can You See Me' by Hendrix?" It had been a number of years, but Chris and I quickly remembered it, and it took no time for Ben and Matt to learn it. I don't know if we ever played it live – we just recorded it for that BBC session…maybe we played it live once, I don't know.

But before we did "Can You See Me," when Hiro [Yamamoto] was in the band, we did "I Don't Live Today." We also used to jam on "Manic Depression" when Hiro was in the band. But curiously, "Manic Depression" was one of Ben Shepherd's favorite songs – I think we probably jammed on it when Ben was in the band, as well. But we never played it live. I do believe we tried "I Don't Live Today" live in some bar in the mid-80's with Hiro and Matt in the band – I was probably drunk and fucked up some parts! [Laughs] But I *love* that song.

Very soulful [is how Kim describes a version of "Hey Baby (Land of the New Rising Sun)," which was covered by Chris Cornell, Matt Cameron, Jeff Ament, and Mike McCready, under the name MACC for 1993's *Stone Free: A Tribute to Jimi Hendrix*]. And I think Chris certainly has a very soulful voice and range that would probably give a new dimension and element to Hendrix's version.

DOUG PINNICK: We were doing the *Dogman* record, and Brendan [O'Brien, producer] said, "Hey, we've got to do a cover. We need one more song for the record." And he said, "How about Jimi Hendrix, 'Manic Depression'?" So, I literally went to the store, bought the record, brought it back, and we played it twice. Went downstairs, and knocked it out in two takes. And then I sang it. The first time I sang it just like Hendrix, and Brendan said, "Hey man...put a little more 'Doug' in it in this second take." So, I kind of did me *and* Jimi – and that's what it was. It was recorded live in the studio, but the audience is actually the Atlanta Rhythm Section audience applause!

It was the only song that woke them up! [When King's X performed "Manic Depression" at Woodstock '94] We did our whole set, and everybody loved it – we had been on MTV, so they had heard of us. But not those many people in the audience probably really paid any attention to us – maybe the songs "It's Love" and "Over My Head." "Over My Head" came off really good – I did the whole speech and everything, which to my surprise, the crowd really responded to. And did a call-back –

I yelled at them and they'd yell back at me.

But when we went into "Manic Depression," the mosh pit happened, and everybody went *nuts*. It was a highlight – the bar was raised. And it kind of saved us – I remember MTV said something like, "King's X came out and did 'Manic Depression,' and just woke everybody up." And they played it – I have a tape of MTV and them talking about it, and then they played the replay of it the next day.

KIRK HAMMETT: Back then [on Metallica's *Damaged Justice* tour, circa 1988-1989], I would do these open guitar solos – mainly to give Lars [Ulrich] and James [Hetfield] a break. And I would go into "Little Wing" to just give that open guitar tone a little more substance – rather than just sit there and show everyone how fast I could play or how many riffs I know. There's a bit more musicality going into "Little Wing." For me, that part was a great way for me to show my respect and appreciation for Jimi Hendrix – as an influence for me. And I always wanted people to know that. He was just a major influence on my guitar style.

BRUCE KULICK: When Gene and Paul wanted me to do a guitar solo…I had to come up with a few different ones through my performing years with Kiss. I couldn't always figure out what would be something exciting to put in the solo – instead of it just being a lot of notes or whatever. But knowing that this performance that Hendrix did [the first time Bruce saw Jimi at MSG] was a lot of improvisation at certain points…in fact, there's a long section where the drums aren't really playing, or he's doing a simple thing behind him, and he's just letting Hendrix create. Because he was at the height of his "I'm just going to improvise here."

And I borrowed some of those riffs that he did [for Bruce's live solo in Kiss] – he would just go off in these interesting chordal patterns and his harmonic structure was something that...I didn't do a *complete* copy, but I borrowed. So, if he went from a chord to a chord to a chord, I took whatever I thought of that, that I could interpret and make my own.

I felt like I found some "gold" that no one else would ever see or mine – and it became part of my live guitar solo. So, not only was that an incredible event to experience, but the fact that I could borrow from that and do things like that at my own Madison Square Garden gig with Kiss – you could see that would be something quite exciting for me.

DOUG PINNICK: Billy Cox, Buddy Miles, Eddie Kramer – I was in a room with all of them one time, doing a Hendrix tribute record a long time ago [on 1995's *In from the Storm: The Music of Jimi Hendrix*, Doug sang lead on a cover of "Burning of the Midnight Lamp," and provided background vocals for "...And the Gods Made Love" and "Have You Ever Been (To Electric Ladyland)"].

And hearing the stories and the vibe that I got from them knowing Jimi, it was pretty overwhelming. He left a big mark on a lot of people. He was bigger than life. They say he was the nicest guy in the world. He was really sweet, and he was very insecure and unsure...but still, did what he did. And his sister [Janie Hendrix], too – just being around these people that knew him or related to him, it gave me an overwhelming sense of what a great guy he was, and how much they really love him.

BRUCE KULICK: Once I knew a little bit production-wise about what the stage [on Kiss' *Revenge* tour] would look like and this Statue of Liberty and everything, I once again went to my hero and thought, "Wouldn't it be great if Kiss did 'The Star-Spangled Banner' at the end of the show?" Paul and I arranged it and it made it to *Alive III* – which is wonderful. And I recently did it on the Kiss Kruise with my band.

But what's really funny is that about four or five years into my career with Grand Funk – I'm into my 20th year now – I remember there was a Memorial Day gig they had, and Don Brewer saying to me, "Bruce, do you know 'The Star-Spangled Banner'? Do you think you can do something with that?" I'm like, "Uh…yeah, I can do that!"

Since then, every night part of the Grand Funk show – when we do the full show – I'm playing "The Star-Spangled Banner." Now, with Grand Funk, I don't even use a guitar with a Floyd Rose or whammy bar or anything – so I'm not doing it real wild or anything. But I'm still doing it – in my mind – very much "Hendrix style."

KIRK HAMMETT: When I bought the *Woodstock* album, there were only two artists I was really interesting in – Santana and Jimi Hendrix. The first thing I did was tape on cassette "The Star-Spangled Banner" and "Villanova Junction" – I would play that day in, day out. I had a tape recorder, and I used to haul this to school with me, and in between classes – and at lunch time – I'd play Jimi Hendrix, "Star-Spangled Banner." And that was a cool thing for me to play at school, because people would go, "Wow! That's 'The Star-Spangled Banner.' Who is that?" *"That's Jimi Hendrix."*

I remember I would come home from school and I'd put it on my dad's stereo and really crank it as loud as possible, and just sit there and swim in the sound of it – because there was just so much *sound* in that version of "The Star-Spangled Banner." And it is the best version of "The Star-Spangled Banner" that Jimi recorded. There have been other versions – a studio version and various other live versions. But the version at Woodstock – to me – is the best version. The most emotional, the one that flows the best, and you're there. *He brings you there.*

We [Kirk and late Metallica bassist Cliff Burton] would sometimes play it together live. And Cliff would play it in E – which is the same key that Jimi played it. But I think the original key for "The Star-Spangled Banner" is in A. It is in A – because I've had to play it at various baseball games and basketball games. When I play it, I'm really tempted to break out Jimi's version – I can do a pretty good job of aping his version and a lot of the fills he plays. And I always offer that to a lot of these sports functions. But they're very conservative – they want "The Star-Spangled Banner" to be played *exactly* as it should be played, with no embellishments or improvisation. People get upset when you alter the form. So, I get up there and play it verbatim.

And at the end, I try to get some sort of feedback or whammy bar action – just as a slight micro-second tribute to Jimi. But you have to play *every single note* correctly. The execution has to be correct and 100%. Because if you mess up one note, everyone knows that you messed up that note – from six year old kids to 96-year-old senior citizens. Everyone knows that melody. *Everyone.*

RON "BUMBLEFOOT" THAL: I did a cover of "Fire" for a Jimi tribute album – *The Spirit Lives On: The Music of Jimi Hendrix Revisited*. It came out in 2004. I just plugged in my fretless, the drummer laid down the drums, I played guitar and bass over it, sang it, and I told the drummer that I'd love to have him doing backing vocals with me. So, he called me up, I let my answering machine get it on cassette, and he sang about ten times on the phone, "Let me stand next to your fire!" I then took the cassette, brought it to the studio, cut them, and put them in as part of the backing vocals.

I actually stole something from "If 6 Was 9" on my first album that I put out on Shrapnel, *The Adventures of Bumblefoot*, called "Q Fever." I had an album called *Normal*, and a song called "Shadow," and that one, the way I'm playing with the double stops and quick grace notes hammered to the actual note…all of that is complete *Jimi thievery*. That guitar phrasing, if I didn't grow up on Jimi Hendrix, I wouldn't have tapped into that part of my own soul and being able to write something like that and play it that way.

Vocally as well, he had the coolness and that swagger. It's storytelling in the way that Jimi told it, it becomes part of your soul, as well. And when you take that in, it becomes part of your DNA, and then when you go to make music, it reveals itself in some way.

CASPAR BRÖTZMANN: There are no songs of me standing in a straight touch and context of a close influence of Hendrix songs – but with a gentle and bigger sense, for sure. I guess all that I ever will play is in a kind of way standing close to my heroes, friends and my living life. With this sense of understanding is the song called "Massaker" – influenced from the whole atmosphere of the Hendrix concert at Woodstock playing "The Star-Spangled Banner." I guess the thing is to find your own way in music to further development, and not to live a life in a shadow like a copy from somebody else.

Jimi Hendrix was my master and this is necessary to talk about, because to learn and watch out and to believe in your own visions and dreams is very important, and this is and can be a very hard and long way to reach and join your own world full of sounds and music you like to play. Hold on to yourself. That is maybe not easy to get there, and a big adventure and challenge to let by side all conditions of a third party were given to you and all the time trying to manipulate to follow them for their own interest. Never give up. Sometimes it will take a long time in a world going faster and faster in crazy times we are in now. These words are also based on my experiences becoming an apprentice and learning carpentry.

KIM THAYIL: Yes, of course. [In response to the question, "Was Jimi's use of feedback an influence on Soundgarden's use of feedback?"] If not directly, then probably within the chain. I mean, you can say the Beatles, the Velvet Underground, the MC5, and Hendrix, then to punk rock and the Sex Pistols, the Dead Boys, Void, the Meat Puppets, Black Flag, Bauhaus, and Soundgarden.

I think in many ways, Hendrix's use of distortion and feedback directly influenced me. Soundgarden is certainly in the chain of bands that used feedback. We used feedback in the songwriting/construction element – not just in the production element. I believe Hendrix did use feedback in the song element and not just the performance element. For example, the song "EXP," off of *Axis: Bold as Love.*

Many producers and engineers thought that feedback and noise reflected poorly on their craft. So, it was really tough. Producers that were musicians – like Jack Endino…or [Soundgarden's soundman] Stuart Hallerman – were certainly encouraging about those elements. But engineers are more into the quality of their craft of recording, and the quality of what goes on tape. They would kind of steer us away from noise and feedback.

But I tried to do it in a way that was manageable, which was contrary to the goal of the noise and feedback – you wanted to embody chaos, you wanted it to be psychedelic, you wanted it to be unpredictable. But I think there is an element of that particular musical aesthetic, which believes you need to master your environment, and the more you master these elements that are difficult to control, the better you are. But then again, you also have surfers that ride the wave.

PAUL LEARY: Oh, absolutely [Jimi was an influence on Paul regarding use of feedback]. That whole thing got worn out pretty quick, but I love that stuff. I remember where I was the first time I heard "The Star-Spangled Banner" recording – I was working at Dairy Queen, and it came over the radio. It was just fun and exciting – especially when you're a young, rebellious kid, and all of a sudden, your guitar can make the most annoying, constant droning, can't-turn-it-off sounds.

The funny thing is back in the day, my parents paid for guitar lessons for me when I was a kid. And the thing I would do is I went to a teacher that I could take any album in there, play a song for him, and he would try and figure it out and play the song. And after doing that for a while, you learned how to do it yourself, and it's not that hard.

All the solos tend to follow a certain scale, and all the chords tend to do a certain thing, and you can just figure it out – it almost becomes kind of predictable after a while. You put on Jimi Hendrix and try and figure that stuff out...and it's just different. It was outside of the mold, for sure. It sounded outside of the mold, but when you tried to play that stuff...*it was different.*

The only name that I can think would be Curt Kirkwood [concerning punk guitarists of the '80s who were influenced by Jimi]. Punk rock was so much barre chords and sheer loudness. There were guitar players that were just turning their instrument into an expressive outlet. For one thing, Curt had a good dynamic range – he could be really powerful and then go to low volumes, clean, and pleasing tones. And then become very unorthodox, and outrageous – all at once.

CURT KIRKWOOD: I was playing quite a bit and I was playing all different kinds of stuff by the time he started to become an influence. And it was never so much technique or sound – it was just abandon interest. *Letting go.* You could tell listening to Jimi that he had the chops to not think about it. So, that was something that I had aspired to. Once we started playing together as a band, we had given ourselves enough freedom to play with that kind of abandon and not think about mistakes or anything else. That was more the influence – just let it rip, play hard.

A pretty big influence on *Up on the Sun*, I would say. I was starting to get into him by then. It took me a little while. I can't say I wasn't familiar…but I just hadn't *absorbed it* – which was probably a godsend, because it might have been intimidating to go through my teens being that into it. It's so good, that it makes you want to quit – even after you get good yourself, why bother? [Laughs] There's only one Jimi Hendrix.

But by the time we did *Up on the Sun*, something like "Pali Gap" would have been an influence there. And just an influence as we became a band in that it was encouraging to see that there was somebody that his intention was to make music like that – that it wasn't an accident. It made me think, "*We're on the right track.*"

EAST BAY RAY: He's definitely an influence on me, but I think in punk rock, I'm very unique sounding. [Laughs] So I don't know. Thinking outside of punk rock, I think the Edge from U2 was influenced by him. When U2 first toured here, they stayed on the floor of a friend's house in San Francisco, so I have a little bit of "brotherhood" with them. They're not really punk rock, but they came out of the same era.

KIM THAYIL: I think his wildness and free spirit would be better embodied with some of the punk rock that would come out later in the '70s. Maybe stuff like the Dead Boys. Certainly stuff like the Stooges and the MC5 – up until '73. After that, the Pistols, Dead Boys, and the Heartbreakers. And talking to you, I know we both like the Meat Puppets! I think *Meat Puppets II.* But there's certainly a plethora of bands in the late '70s...the guitarist Daniel Ash from Bauhaus, on the album *In the Flat Field* is amazingly wild and certainly not afraid of feedback.

But certainly Nirvana – the way Kurt [Cobain] approached his guitar emotively and the feedback, and not afraid of pushing his ability and embracing the chaos and noise. But guitarists also showing a technical ability and proficiency...God, it's tough. Adrian Belew, Paul Leary of the Butthole Surfers...I think there's a lot of Seattle bands – Steve Turner of Mudhoney has done stuff like that, I think I've done stuff like that, I think Buzz Osborne from the Melvins. Neil Young used feedback and noise in cool ways – but he may not have been fast and proficient in a "guitar god way" that fret-heads may be into.

I think there are metalheads that embrace the proficient and technical aspect of what Hendrix could do – and often did. There are blues guys that embrace the soulful and emotive side of what Hendrix did. There are punk rock guys that embraced the wildness and energy of what Hendrix did – I might reference the song "Who Are You," the first song off the split Faith/Void single, on the Void side. My buddy Bubba Dupree, the way he played guitar on that, it's got a nice, wild, on-the-verge-of-tearing-apart sort of sound to it. I think it's almost as if what Hendrix brought to the electric guitar in rock n' roll split things into "metal" and "punk" ethics or ethos.

CASPAR BRÖTZMANN: Yes, I think so. [In response to the question "Were you inspired to form the trio Caspar Brötzmann Massaker because of the same trio set-up of the Jimi Hendrix Experience and Band of Gypsys?"] I'm pretty sure about this. But also, it is a personal thing for me, the constellation of three people. This is a good circle and feeling.

But please don't forget, I started with Deep Purple and Led Zeppelin and played in a punk band. I was not trying to be the same as Hendrix. It is since today a misunderstanding that people think, "Oh wow; left-hand Strat and Marshall stacks...oh yeah, he is doing like Hendrix." It's not, and I didn't care about it for a long time. We played a few times in Seattle and had no problems at all with comparing Hendrix to Massaker, and in the end why not? It would be a great compliment.

ANDY GILL [Gang of Four guitarist]: "It's complicated yet simple" is the sort of dumb answer [to how Andy created his guitar style], because there were so many types of music I loved. When I was young, Hendrix was a big obsession, with his flowing, soloing, colorful, expressive style. But there were more groove-orientated things that got me quite excited – a lot of Motown things which are not guitar-driven at all. With Motown, the way the grooves were put together really got under my skin.

And people like Steve Cropper, who is an amazing, underrated rhythm guitarist. Nile Rodgers is a descendent of Cropper in a way – someone who totally knows their chords but has got an incredible rhythmic feel. That very-rhythmic thing, abstract feedback, and those drones, again – a bit on the Hendrix side of things; if you like, a very "paint-ily" approach to making noise on the guitar.

And then reggae and that feeling for space – it's the antithesis of all those rock guitarists who are throwing as many notes as possible in their solos. Reggae is the kind of antidote for that. I didn't really like any punk guitarists at all, but the great pre-punk Dr. Feelgood – Wilko Johnson was an enormous influence on me. Listen to "Damaged Goods" and you know where that kind of vibe comes from. It's all over the place.*

EAST BAY RAY: I originally started with a Telecaster with humbucking pickups in it. The Strat was the other one Fender made, and it has the whammy bar on it. I think the song "Halloween," where I use the whammy bar...Jimi Hendrix was an influence on that, too – he used the tremolo bar a lot. But I can't remember why I got a Strat. [Laughs] But I think the fact that he played one.

*Quote is from the *Vintage Guitar* article, *Andy Gill: The Gang's All Here*, by Greg Prato (January 2017).

Syd Barrett played a Telecaster, so you might be right – subconsciously, it was there.

CASPAR BRÖTZMANN: There was a music store in my home city. A half year before my 18th birthday, they placed in the main front window a brand new black left-hand Stratocaster with a maple neck and big head stock. The day of my birthday, I ran into the shop and bought the guitar with a bank credit. My single one in life.

A dream was coming true, because I was anxious a half year long, that somebody else would buy the guitar earlier as I could do. What a great moment this was – my 18th birthday, 1980. About pros and cons – I have only pros and no cons with my left-hand Fender Stratocaster. If I had the choice, I always would take a left-hand Strat, because the whole body feeling is dazzling.

I started with a Pearl copy of a right-hand Fender Strat and played this guitar from 14 to 18 years old, because I was a fan of Blackmore. I had no idea about Hendrix in my early beginning to play electric guitar. Led Zeppelin was my next favorite band. Both bands used a lot of Marshall stacks. They all used the Super Lead 100-watt Plexi amps modified or not, and so that's the reason I thought this would be also a good idea for me to do.

I had four years' experience to play a regular right-hand Strat before I changed over to play a left-hand Strat like a right-handed man. To have the volume/tone controls, the pickup switcher, and tremolo bar more superior at the pick guard plate is really great and comfortable for me. Again, the left-hand Fender Stratocaster is the perfect guitar for me.

With a left-hand, the controls are now more under my right wrist joint and the space below is free to hit the strings in any way smooth and strong. You have a free feeling to play if the controls are away. And you can so easily hit the edge of cabs with the guitar body to get the real deep bass inferno feedback. Some other guitar players maybe would say that it is difficult to play the neck at the last higher frets, because the guitar body was not so deep countersunk for the left hand. It doesn't matter for me.

One of the best pros is for my feeling, that the mechanics on the neck placed on the underside and the best anyway of all is that the guitar body has the short side now on your ribs, that feels much more flexible and made the whole handling of the guitar much better in an easygoing way.

More specific details – the position of the bridge pickup is turned over now and not that close to the bridge and sound has a bit less treble for the higher strings G / B / E. And the deep E-string has a longer distance between the saddle and mechanics at the head stock. If you hit this string at the headstock you can have beautiful sounds. This only works with a left-hand Strat playing by a right hand.

ALEX LIFESON: His playing was not as direct an influence as other guitarists of that time, for me, but I always respected everything about his playing. When Rush first started gigging in 1968, "Purple Haze" and "Hey Joe" were in our original set list – soon followed by "Fire," "Foxy Lady," and an attempt at "Manic Depression."

KK DOWNING: My general subconscious feeling, as I go into a certain mode and I do certain things – especially when I improvise – and I use the wah pedal and the tremolo arm and stuff like that, then Hendrix is alive in me in that way. I have that *feeling* about him – without wanting to copy any of his chops. Other players have had so-called "songs of Hendrix." And I'm not going to deny that really, in fact, I feel very proud of that, really – there are certain players that carry on the light, without copying. Hendrix to me was unsurpassable at what he did, anyway. But this is what people often do – they influence other musicians.

I'm lucky to have been on the planet long enough to have had so many great performing artists walk in the dressing room and they say that they were inspired by me and Judas Priest. And that's great to hear from great players. And they can be from any band...really top well-known people, and certain people you wouldn't think – the guys in Slipknot, for example. Machine Head said they grew up on Priest. And Slayer. The younger fraternity, as well, of players – which is all very rewarding, really.

FRANK MARINO: I did say at one point – when all that Hendrix stuff was going on – "One day, Jimi Hendrix's guitar playing is going to be the standard by which all guitar players will be judged." I said that to people that were telling me that wasn't true. And I said, "You'll see. That's going to be the barometer." And it *did* become the barometer.

I didn't say that because I knew the future, I said that because it just seemed obvious to me that it would. And it did – only after he died. Because had it not been for those people that took the bad Jimi Hendrix bootlegs and put out all those posthumous bad releases, Jimi Hendrix probably would have faded away. That would have happened.

But there was this constant glut of *Crash Landing* and all off these albums that I can't remember the guy's name who owned the rights to that stuff [Alan Douglas], but he kept putting out one bad bootleg after another. I think there are only two tracks on posthumous releases that were worthy of Jimi Hendrix, and that's on the record *Hendrix in the West* – with his versions of "Red House" and "Little Wing." I think pretty much a lot of that other stuff...how many times can you have Jimi playing "Hear My Train A Comin'" and "Blue Suede Shoes" – from a bad board mix?

MICHAEL SCHENKER: Jimi Hendrix didn't inspire me for anything, actually, because he bypassed. It's a bit like, there are some people that later I started to understand, because I started to focus on them – once I was done with the stuff that I really liked. But I was intrigued into aggressive music.

Actually, who inspired me with the wah wah pedal – if anybody – was Mick Ronson...or the guy from Humble Pie [Peter Frampton or Clem Clempson]. I think it was Mick Ronson I heard, because I became a David Bowie fan, and Mick Ronson was playing a wah wah. And the sound of it was like...*soaring*. It added something to it. And Jeff Beck too, of course. More of them.

STEVE VAI: Well, it's impossible to escape his influence – and any guitar player that's ever heard him. It's impossible to fully escape the influence of any guitar player you've ever heard. It just works itself in there somehow. With someone like Hendrix, probably more so than other players – because we sit there and try to learn that stuff.

But let me answer the question…yeah, virtually every solo would sound different – if it was a solo at all – if Hendrix never was. If he never was, I don't know if I'd be doing a solo. Who knows? But if I did, it would be very different. I'm sure that guitar aficionados would understand this – every guitar player that puts their fingers on the instrument, there's a sound that comes out that is unique to that player.

The analogy I use is there are no two snowflakes that are exactly the same – that's supposed to be a factual statistic. Though it would stand to reason that no two notes that anyone plays is the same – the personality is in the way you play. And Hendrix, his perspective of music and the world and his intentions – his perspective on his own intentions – were very powerful and focused. And he knew what he wanted. Those intentions flowed out through his fingers. And as a result, you get what you hear when you listen to Hendrix.

And how many times have you heard guitar players try to sound like Hendrix? They can get *sort of* close, but nobody is ever going to sound like that. And nobody is going to ever sound like those who are trying to sound like Hendrix. But…there's an energy in Jimi's playing that is infectious and inspiring – because it just resonated from a different dimension than most people expressed through. He just had a different vision. So, that energy is what I try to capture. That is what flowed into my playing and I believe what flows into a lot of guitar player's playing.

You may not hear me playing something and go, "Oh…that's Hendrix. That's the most 'Hendrix' guitar solo I've ever heard Vai do." You may not hear that because I don't choose those notes – my fingers don't work that way. I'm very much attracted to the things he played. But I'm more attracted to the things I play, obviously – or else I'd be playing his music. But that energy, that overview, that command, that "I don't give a fuck attitude" – that was what was most inspiring to me. I mean, I can say, "Yeah, this song you can hear the vibrato in my solo that came from Hendrix, or the whammy bar riff here." I can point out various things, but it's the overall energy in my solos that I strive for – that I believe is most connected to Hendrix.

But perhaps something like "Gravity Storm" – that's pretty "Hendrix-y." Although, it's got time signatures and shit in it. If I find myself trying to play like, "Red House," I feel really out of sorts – it just doesn't feel right to me, to try to play like that or have that "authentic blues Hendrix sound." Because first of all, why? He already did it. And second of all, I can't. It's not in my wheelhouse. It's too…not to sound pretentious, but it's too conventional and it gets watered down, and sounds like bad white boy blues – for decades. I just don't want to be that. Because if I try to play authentic blues, I would sound like a bad white boy.

DOUG PINNICK: When I got the opportunity to make that [2018's *Tribute to Jimi (Often Imitated But*

Never Duplicated)], I had to decide how I wanted to do it. Because everybody does Hendrix, and everybody does tribute records. I thought, "How can I make this stand out and do something that's not like everybody else?" On this record, I thought, "What would Jimi do, if Jimi had to go in the studio and re-do a bunch of songs?" He'd probably go in there and go so far from the original that we wouldn't even recognize them, because he'd be 50 years older now. He'd probably be so far beyond that.

So, I thought, "Well, why don't I do the opposite? Why don't I do stuff *exactly* – that's the challenge." So, we did – we literally got the guitars, the amps, the pedals, everything we could think of, and put those records on, and played them over and listened. And Michael Parnin – the producer – and I painstakingly just tried to find every little nuance.

I play guitar and bass on that record and sang, and Mike Hansen played drums, and Tracey Singleton played all the leads, because I didn't want to attempt Jimi's leads – I'm not a lead player. But, people say that I sound like Jimi when I play leads, because...I sound like a drunk Jimi Hendrix! You can go, "Oh, he sounds like Hendrix...but he ain't on it." [Laughs] I can get that tone, I can make it scream, but I don't know what I'm doing. So, even to this day, I can listen to it and go, "We did pretty good."

And here's the weirdest thing now – doing these two Hendrix tribute tours, they play Hendrix between sets all day. And every now and then, I walk in the building, and I go, "Who's that? That sounds like me. Oh...*it's Jimi.*" I am so used to my voice sounding like Jimi, that sometimes, I can't tell them apart. I'll put Jimi Hendrix on in the house, and I'll go, "Fuck, that sounds like me." I'm like, "Damn, I get it." Because if I can hear it, then it must freak people out. I know people that said that I kind of scare them sometimes. I can do Phil Lynott just like Phil Lynott, too.

CURT KIRKWOOD: I probably didn't learn it the right way! [When the Meat Puppets covered "Little Wing" live back in the '80s] I doubt I played it right from the get-go – I'm bad that way. It's hard for me to learn stuff…unless it's a country song.

ADRIAN BELEW: Jimi's style of chording, his radical use of effects, and his apparent curiosity about sounds have been subtly ever present in so much of what I try to do. Not to copy him – who could? But to hopefully sprinkle a little bit of his magic into my creations. It's part of my musical DNA – just like the Beatles are. If I could point to one song of mine: "Phone Call from the Moon" would suffice. But there are many other examples.

BRUCE KULICK: Not only that live solo thing I was telling you from my Kiss years that I borrowed things that aren't really well-known – things that he kind of improvised that day – but I know in "Jungle," my solo is a little between a Hendrix and Clapton homage. Certainly, some of the whammy bar things that I'd be doing – more likely on *Revenge*. The fact that I hinted at "The Star-Spangled Banner" on "Spit" – that's obviously a tip of the hat to Hendrix.

If I'm playing really aggressively with a wah and distortion – which was not always on the Kiss recordings, but certainly we know a few records that feature that – I'm obviously thinking "Hendrix." On *Carnival of Souls* there is a particular Strat sound on "In the Mirror" that is very Hendrix-like. All the backwards stuff in "I Walk Alone" from *Carnival of Souls* – that's a Strat and that's done totally influenced by how Hendrix did backwards guitars, and how you have to kind of map out thinking backwards when you're playing along with the tape forward. The tape is backward, you have to play it forward, and then the reverse happens – and there's that backwards solo. And even though they offer some pedals that mimic some of that behavior of a guitar – by the swell of it – it's not the same.

And not only in solos did he influence me, but there were so many tones and techniques on the guitar and pedals that would be chosen for certain albums – especially during my Kiss years and beyond. I'd have to admit that even on my solo records there are a lot of those kind of techniques that I've mentioned – on *BK3* especially. But even on the other two solo records [2001's *Audiodog* and 2003's *Transformer*]. And the song with Gene ["Ain't Gonna Die" on *BK3*] I think had some aggressive Strat and whammy soloing things. Sometimes, even composition-wise, like there's some moving basslines on a track ["I'm the Animal"], where that's *totally* influenced from Jimi Hendrix. He's been a huge influence for me.

I almost feel embarrassed by if I actually examine any of those albums or works that I did, that easily I maybe can point to as much of 50% of that stuff and I can show you something that was Hendrix-related. Even that ESP/Eric Singer Project album that I did, we covered "Changes" [on 1999's

ESP] – Karl Cochran sang it so well. On that record we did "Foxy Lady" and Ace was the special guest. And I'll give you another one – Ace is putting out another record, and on that record, "Manic Depression" was covered by him, and I'm playing lead guitars with him. So, there you go – *another* Kiss connection with Hendrix!

DOUG PINNICK: Our thing was to just not go out and be ourselves and do Hendrix songs like a lot of people have done in the past [when Doug played with Joe Satriani and Kenny Aronoff as part of the Experience Hendrix Tour in 2019]. We thought we would go out there and try to reconstruct the songs in the essence of the way Jimi did it. So, we went out and tried to do Jimi live, basically. If you went to see Hendrix brash, loud, chaotic, and in-your-face – that's what we did. When we went on stage, people said it went up *eight notches*. And we slammed these people until the end. It was a lot of fun.

Kenny overplayed Mitch Mitchell to the point where it was like chaos sometimes. Me and Joe would just go, "I don't know where he's at...but we'll just find our way sooner or later." And Joe's playing, he never did any "Satriani" at all – he did *all* Hendrix. He did blues and his best renditions of Hendrix on every song – it was really fun to do. I went out there to do my Hendrix, and they said, "This is when you can go *all the way*, Doug." So, I did.

I probably not only sounded like him, but tried to sing somewhat what he was thinking. How he felt about the song. Because I had to marry the lyrics – I'd get up there and sing them and play them. So, all of a sudden, I'm realizing, "Will I live tomorrow? Well I just can't say. But I know for sure I don't live today." I'm going, "*Wow.*"

Because it's not like, "My baby left me," it's really deep. It's like, what is he trying to say? Is he saying that somebody is going to kill him? Or is he just depressed enough to kill himself? But any way you want to put it, they were very simple and very direct to my heart. And there are a lot of times I'm standing in front of a microphone, singing "No sun coming through my windows, Feel like I'm sitting at the bottom of a grave" – and I feel like that. And it came out in my voice. "I wish you'd hurry up and execute me, So I can be on my miserable way" – it's not just "way," it's "*miserable* way." It's so etched in my heart. People say that I can sing the telephone book like Jimi. And I'm happy I can do that for them.

Playing-wise, all I can say is Billy Cox [who was also part of the Experience Hendrix tour that Doug was on] sounds like he did before – he's a great bass player. There's nothing I can say other than he played the bass, he played the riffs, and he had the magic that he had. And the stories that he told me about Jimi, he'd just nonchalantly talk about Jimi and the things that they did – "Jimi said, 'Little Richard needs a bass player, come play with us. I'm leaving tomorrow'." And Billy said, "Well, I can't leave tomorrow – I have a job. I have to tie things up – give me a week." And Little Richard said, "No, you've got to go *now*." And Jimi left – Billy missed that gig. But Billy said, "But I'm a responsible guy. I take care of things and I want respect."

And that's one of the things I learned about him – he didn't have all these stories about being drunk all the time and not remembering anything like most of those cats. He had all those stories, because he was always sober – which is really, really cool about him. And he's still here because of it, too. He's healthy as a racehorse – he turned 80 on this tour. The highlight to me is getting to meet him, and knowing that that's the guy that I learned how to play bass from.

He came up to me and said, "Man, I like the way you sound. What are you playing through?" And I said, "It's my dUg pedal [by Tech 21]. Go on YouTube and look up the 'DP-3X'." And he comes up to me the next day, and says, "I got everything I needed to know. I got *two* of them!" And after every show, he'd come up to me and say, "Man, you've got some fire in you – you're a badass bass player. I've been learning a thing or two from you." And I'm going, "I learned everything from *you*!"

Taj Mahal did the same thing, he said, "I'm a bass player, man. That's what I do. I play guitar and sing blues, but I'm really a bass player. I hate bass players that play with a pick…but you're the only bass player with a pick that's badass!" That whole tour was fun, because you're hanging with a whole bunch of really great musicians. It was everyone listening to each other and complimenting each other. It was a lot of fun.

BRUCE KULICK: Paul Stanley and I used to talk about Hendrix quite a bit. He'd do the scratch thing on the guitar like "Are You Experienced." Gene, we both loved that kind of music – there's no doubt. I think out of all the guys, Paul had the definite connection. Now, you know Ace loved Hendrix. And Ace and I have talked about it quite a few times. So,

I think having Ace in that band – even though he doesn't really sound anything like Hendrix, he was known for a Les Paul – he hasn't denied his influence that Jimi Hendrix and Jimmy Page were probably the top two. And it's pretty obvious – for sure.

REVEREND HORTON HEAT: Stevie Ray Vaughan, Robin Trower [are the top "Hendrix disciples"]. That being said, those are more direct influences. But he had an influence on everybody, pretty much. In some ways, it caused some people to go in reverse – I think Eric Clapton…Eric Clapton was the guy that brought the concept of string bending to our consciousness. When he first came to America, I think Clapton saw Hendrix, and said, "*Man.*"

Instead of doing the Cream style thing, I think he said, "I'm just going to be doing rootsy blues." Clapton kind of backed it down from the Les Paul through Marshall sound…or the big guitar sound went back down to bluesy Strat tones. But when you consider that, he influenced everybody – Eric Clapton, Pete Townshend…*everybody.*

FRANK MARINO: I thought it was a little bit odd because I knew Robin Trower beforehand – and it wasn't influenced that way. He had been the guitar player for Procol Harum. So, if you listen to "Shine on Brightly," "A Whiter Shade of Pale," or whatever, it's not exactly the same kind of guitar sound or the same kind of guitar approach. So, when Robin began to do the other approach, I thought, "Well, there's definitely a marked change in a person's approach. Obviously, he's made a decision to approach guitar in a different way." I happen to think it's the right way to do it.

RICHARD LLOYD: There's a million of them. But I think of John Frusciante of the Red Hot Chili Peppers – he's very Hendrix-oriented. John Mayer did a version of "Wait Until Tomorrow." Stevie Ray Vaughan was a total copy of Jimi – I mean, Jimi and the blues connected. But a tremendous influence there. Carlos Santana was definitely influenced by Jimi – although he was already a great guitar player at Woodstock. So, I don't know how much he was influenced by Jimi's stuff before that, but I know that afterwards, he always claimed Jimi as being an influence. The list goes on and on.

CASPAR BRÖTZMANN: I think there are still many guitar players using feedback for their playing. Sunn O))) for example, sounds like moving monstrous feedback mountains.

STEVE VAI: I don't think that Prince was able to escape that influence, either. When you heard Hendrix play, it was so easy to say, "OK. That is where I want to go…or at least start from…or at least incorporate into my playing." And I see that in Prince, too. Prince I believe is an underrated guitar player. He was very capable. I've seen him do certain jams and stuff that were real wonderful – they were very explorative and connected. That's the side of Prince's guitar playing that I really loved. And I really loved and learned from his rhythm playing – he was as solid as you can be, man. *He was like a funk machine.*

KIRK HAMMETT: Uli Jon Roth and Stevie Ray Vaughan. Those guys are both in my top tier of influence – especially Uli. Uli for me, he started doing something that resonated with me completely. He took that Jimi Hendrix approach/attack…that sound, that attitude, and meshed it with a classical approach. A very modal sort of approach. And throwing in arpeggios. Not three string arpeggios, but full arpeggiated chords over six tones, instead of the standard three.

Up to that point, a lot of arpeggios that were being played in rock music were just three tones. But Uli was playing six tone arpeggios and playing them *super* fast. He was the first guy I heard do that – outside of jazz and traditional classical music. And when Uli did that – and blended that classical attitude with the Jimi Hendrix attitude – he turned it into some other thing. It was an amazing result. Uli sort of led me down that same path – learn Jimi Hendrix stuff and apply it to what you already know, and see what comes out. And that's basically what I did. It's kind of a microcosm of what Uli did.

Moving on to Stevie Ray Vaughan, if you listen to Stevie's solos, it's really interesting – because a lot of times, in the middle of the solo, all of a sudden, I'll hear Hendrix licks. I'm like, "Oh my God…he's playing verbatim a Jimi solo!" *Verbatim.* The best example is one time I was watching Stevie, and then he starts aping the small little solo section at the end of the last song on the *Band of Gypsys* album. I totally caught it, and I was like, "Wow…he's playing that outro solo on that song from *Band of Gypsys*!"

I loved that Stevie was able to figure out a lot

of the things that Jimi did – sound-wise. Like, at the beginning of "Foxy Lady," that feedback. That "scratching string sound" that you hear before the feedback comes in…I wasn't exactly sure how Jimi Hendrix did that. But then, I saw Stevie Ray do it – and all he was doing was just rubbing the string against the neck, and shaking it while he was not picking it with his right hand. And *that's* how he got the sound. And there are other sounds and other ways that he got that Jimi Hendrix-type thing going. A lot of times, he would fit simple octave minor chords into the solos – the way Jimi Hendrix would.

RON "BUMBLEFOOT" THAL: Hell, I mean, who *wasn't* influenced by him! I think every guitar player was. Stevie Ray Vaughan was different. Yeah, he played a Stratocaster and he played blues rock, but he had his own personality – he had his own hat, his own tone. To me, Hendrix was more of this free spirit and Stevie Ray was a more technical player…but a cleaner, more southern rock, a little bit country, blues hybrid player.

To me, I think Jimi was an influence – he influenced me and he influenced everybody in some way. But I wouldn't look at Stevie and say, "He stole his persona from Jimi Hendrix." Sure, there's some influence there, but I could play you songs right now where the guitar approach is completely Jimi Hendrix – myself – but nobody is going to look at me and say, "Oh, he's a Jimi disciple." But Jimi, definitely the way he played – his phrasing, tone, everything – is absolutely…it became a building block and some sort of influential piece for every rock guitar player out there.

CURT KIRKWOOD: Probably an influence on anybody that came after him. It's pretty hard to avoid when you're a guitar player and once you get into it and realize how broad a range of sounds guitars can make.

KIRK HAMMETT: I've consistently listened to Jimi Hendrix pretty much all my life! Just yesterday, I was listening to the newest one, *Songs for Groovy Children.* And all those reissues…I'm a sucker – I'm *still* buying them. I can't help myself.

Chapter 7
Frank Marino Dispels
"The Jimi Myth"

Remember the tale concerning Jimi's spirit teaching
Frank how to play guitar during a hospital stay?

FRANK MARINO: This is such a ridiculous story, and I was saying it the day it came out – *when* it came out! And no one ever listened. It's like…you talk and you talk and you talk and they go, "Oh yeah, that's nice" – but they don't listen. Because they love the story, they loved the narrative. But my logic – and it really *is* logic – is yes, I did go to a hospital. And yes, I did go through a terribly bad trip. And yes, I did learn to play guitar in the hospital. And yes, I did play Jimi Hendrix-style music. But I did that in September of 1968! Jimi Hendrix died in September of 1970 – *a full two years later*. So, the idea that there was some kind of reincarnation experience in the hospital – which is how the story is framed – is absolutely ridiculous if you can say it, because of the year difference.

    This was just one single writer's tongue-in-cheek, snide remark, that magazines picked up and ran with – without even bothering to look at the facts. And at the time that they did run with it, I was only just getting started in the music businesses, so it wasn't like they knew what to call me. No one ever called me about that. So, I would try to tell people – the people who were my managers at the time – "Can you please tell these people to knock this off?" All I ever heard was "Hendrix, Hendrix, Hendrix" –

forever and ever. And yes, OK, I dedicated my first album "To the memory of Jimi Hendrix" – like anyone would do when an artist has just died and you've just made an album. Which is exactly what happened – I wrote a song called "Buddy" about Jimi Hendrix, and it's dedicated to Jimi Hendrix.

It wasn't so much the press, but it was the rock magazines like *Circus* and *Creem*. They were the ones that perpetuated this, and then local newspapers would start picking up this story. And it went from "reincarnation in the hospital" to "a car accident" to "a coma" – all kinds of stuff. And I just never stopped hearing the name Jimi Hendrix for the rest of my career – to today. So, that's what I meant about the irony about being the guy who walked out on him. I mean, it wouldn't be ironic if I wasn't so associated in that way.

There are out there certain articles that I didn't manage to get into print – as early as '71/'72/'73 – dispelling this. But no one ever talks about that. They seem to think that *I'm* the guy who said all these things. And it got so bad that I began to ironically joke about it. That whole thing, *Child of the Novelty*, is a tongue-in-cheek reference to what people were saying. And I have a song on there called "Talkin' 'bout a Feelin'," which goes, "People put me down like I'm doing something sacred, blah blah blah…leave me alone." I'm basically saying that in the song. It's not like I didn't acknowledge that this shit was going down, but listen man, you can't argue with people who buy ink by the barrel. You just won't win that argument.

And it's interesting because an article just came out now in England – in a magazine called

Rock Candy – there's a spread inside about me, and on the cover it says, "Frank Marino: 'Enough with the Hendrix already'!" [Laughs] Even Wikipedia has me dispelling it, but it never catches on, man. I don't know why. I guess some people like to play that narrative, and that's more important than the fact. But I genuinely *don't* like it.

Chapter 8
"How hard is it for you to sound like Jimi Hendrix without playing a Jimi Hendrix song?"

When legendary filmmaker Francis Ford Coppola hired Randy Hansen to compose music for his now-classic 1979 film, Apocalypse Now, *he had a specific sound in mind...*

RANDY HANSEN: I'm probably the best known "Jimi Hendrix guy" out there, and I've done other things – I've done work on *Apocalypse Now* and soundtracks. Francis Ford Coppola originally wanted to try and find some unused Jimi stuff. But then he found out that it was going to cost him too much, so he wanted to see if there was somebody else out there in the world that could sound like Jimi Hendrix. The story I got – Francis told me this – was that his daughter pointed out that I was coming to San Francisco, and going to play at the Old Waldorf, and it advertised me as a tribute to Jimi Hendrix. He thought, "Hmmm...I wonder if this guy can do it?"

He got ahold of management through the advertisement, and then they got ahold of us on the road, and gave me a date to get on an airplane to go meet with him at his restaurant that he owned in downtown San Francisco. I met him there, but nobody sold me in on Francis Ford Coppola – I'd just heard his name once. But I didn't know who he was at all. So, I went there not knowing who he was, and he's got on a t-shirt and he looked like Brutus – from *Popeye*. I was sitting there with him, and he goes, "How hard is it for you to sound like Jimi Hendrix without playing a Jimi Hendrix song?" I said, "It's no problem." I was really cocky about it, because I thought, "This guy is putting together some tiny little movie." I couldn't believe that I had to go through an actual audition. So, he goes, "OK. It pays double-scale…do you want it?" I said, "Yeah, I'll do it."

When I came to town, I thought I'd be staying at a hotel. Instead, he had me staying at *his house* with him! So, I woke up every morning having breakfast with the Coppola family – which meant his dad, his wife, and his children. And every morning, his dad would play the piano and start composing new music. He did that every day – he would get a stack of music paper and just fill it with music, and give it to a recordist, who would go on a piano and record everything that he wrote. He would have a tape of it, so it sounded the way it did in his head. And he did that a lot.

That was my wake-up every morning, and then we would go and Francis would roll me a couple of joints. We would smoke a couple of joints together, and then he would roll me a couple of joints and leave a bunch of weed there for me, and then I would just record all day long – looking at different scenes and trying to depict what was going on, on the screen.

Eventually, I told him, "I'm having difficulty doing this. I need to know what's really going on in the scene – what is the feeling going on? If you show me what you have of the movie…" And he said ok. He had a theater in his basement, so he showed me the whole movie down there, and on my way down there to the basement, I noticed a closet door opened where the water heater was, and there was a Rickenbacker bass laying on the ground in the case – open.

I went and watched the movie, came back out, went back in to record, and he said, "Is there anything else I can get you?" And I said, "Yeah. Get me a bass guitar." He goes, "OK. I'll rent one for you." And I go, "No – you've got one in your basement!" He goes, "*Oh yeah.*" So, I played that. That was in the longest scene that I did – it was in a scene that we weren't even supposed to be working on. And when he found out that we had just finished working on that scene, he hit the roof. He started yelling at the producer, David Rubinson, "You know how far over budget I am right now, and you're working on scenes that are *already* filled?!" Then he said, "Since you did it, I want to see what you did."

They roll it, he sits motionless, and watches the entire thing. And this is the longest scene in the movie – continuous scene – it's right where Chief gets speared, and he's being buried by the hippie guy, Lance. But anyway, they're burying him in the water, and then they continue on, and the next scene is when they're arriving at Kurtz's compound. They're going down the river, so, I'm playing the bass, going, "Bom bom…bom bom…bom bom." And it has all this weird, eerie guitar shit that I put in alongside of it. And then the other effects that were already in the regular soundtrack – the sound of the water and the boat going really slow, and the boat rudder and all that is in there, too.

So, he watched that and listened, and then the

scene is over, and he turns to me, and he goes, "That was fucking great! Y'know what? I'm going to use that." I just breathed a sigh of relief, because before, I was like, "I'm going to be fired." I went, "*Pheeew*!" Then nervously, I said, "I really like that bass." He goes, "I'll tell you what…I'll give it to you." I still have it, it's a Rickenbacker 4000 – *it's something that Chris Squire would have drooled over*.

Chapter 9
Changing The Course

Has there been another guitarist since Jimi that immediately changed the course of rock guitar?

KK DOWNING: Definitely not for me. Even the greats that saw Jimi, before you knew it, Pete Townshend was smashing his guitar on stage, and they smashed all of their gear up. The influence... everybody probably would have gone, "I want to do that." Even the likes of probably Clapton and Jeff Beck. It was all about playing, but Jimi came along and said, "No guys. You play not just great – better than great – but you've also got to *perform* better than great." And that is what Hendrix had – that the other guys didn't have. And that rubbed off on me, as well – as soon as I saw Jimi, I said, "Hey guys, we've got to perform. Just playing great is not good enough. You have to put on *a show and a performance.*"

Hendrix went out there as a three-piece – but it was like watching a dozen people on stage performing. Hendrix was so charismatic, with the moves and everything he did in his heyday. And obviously, Priest went out there to do strong, big shows – lots of energy and lots of performance. I took that on board, as well. Some bands haven't, but some bands have. If you go see Iron Maiden, for example, apart from the songs, the legacy, and the playing, you'll see *a show*. And these are the bands that people want to pay to go see. You'll see bands that a lot of people don't think play that great, but they certainly cover it up with a great performance and show.

RIK EMMETT: No. And there never will be again, because the market has become too fragmented, and the social demographics of things and the culture is so very different. The other thing is that nowadays, we have so many guitar players with such incredible specialized techniques – I'm thinking about guys that can do hammer-on kind of things and at the same time they're playing bass with the heel of their hand!

There is stuff going on now, and they'll get millions of hits on YouTube, and it's a counterculture that exists, where technique is raised to insane levels. But, that remains kind of a "YouTube thing." It's not like it's in the mass market. And it's not that those guys are going to get to be on *Ed Sullivan* on Sunday night. The world was a different world then. So, Hendrix took it by storm, because he was this wild man on guitar, who was setting it on fire, and all these kinds of things.

You're probably right about Eddie Van Halen [being the only other guitarist on par with Jimi, concerning changing the course of rock guitar] – certainly from a guitar player perspective. Just guitar culture. It was a ground shift when Eddie happened. But he wasn't a *whole culture* kind of thing. The Beatles wore *Sgt. Pepper's* stuff, but Hendrix had done it first – he had those kind of military jacket things, and then *everybody* wanted those military jackets.

I don't think when Van Halen happened everybody was running out to get chaps without a bum in them. [Laughs] I don't mean to discredit Eddie at all – because that was David Lee Roth's thing – but Van Halen didn't necessarily totally change the entire culture. Like fashion, and all those kinds of things. But from guitar playing, you're probably right about Eddie. That's probably true.

BRIAN TATLER: I think he is the most influential guitarist of all-time. Yeah, Van Halen has been probably #2, but no, I think everybody got something from Hendrix. It certainly became a really, really powerful lead instrument, and we've all followed his lead, really.

ADRIAN BELEW: Sure, there are others, not all of them rock guitarists, of course. But Jimi was the one who shocked us all, pushed us in a new direction, and did things no one else will ever do. Personally, I have to say my favorite guitar player is still Jeff Beck, because over his lifetime, he changed just as much for the guitar community – maybe more. But he did it over a course of *decades* – Jimi only had three or four years.

So, Jimi was the bigger shock to everyone, but in fact, I think in the end, Jeff Beck added more to the world of guitar...or at least as much. I would have to say that – to me, they're equals. I suppose it's an unfair comparison to begin with, because Jimi was a songwriter and a singer and kind of a "freak performer." Jeff Beck is more of a pure guitar player.

DOUG PINNICK: Maybe not like Jimi did, but there are guitarists that changed the course of rock n' roll. Jimi basically pulled the veil up from over our eyes, and said, "*Look what you can do,*" and then he let us run. Like, Eddie Van Halen took some of those things and made a whole career out of it. I think Jimi Hendrix and the Beatles and Led Zeppelin are three artists that you can always get inspired by – if you put their records on and listen to how they wrote songs, how they delivered them, their adventurousness in how they did it, and how great the songs were at the time.

CHEETAH CHROME: Let me think...y'know, Lou Reed, the New York Dolls, James Williamson, and Ron Asheton sure seem to come to mind!

KIM THAYIL: Certainly you can say that about George Harrison and John Lennon. Personally, Jeff Beck is my favorite guitarist ever...but I don't know if he had as dramatic an influence on rock music or commercial rock music as Hendrix may have had. But while Hendrix was doing what he was doing, there was also the MC5 and the Velvet Underground. So, I think that Hendrix's success is what those other bands – like the Sonics, the MC5, or the Velvet Underground – may have lacked.

The song "I Feel Fine" by the Beatles is often referred to as the earliest recorded document of feedback in a song. I'm sure there's feedback in a lot of rawer and cheaper productions...back in the '50s or early '60s are often one-take recordings. And I'm sure if you're going to do a one-take recording, you're going to get some mess-ups and noise throughout, and feedback appearing in some of these situations.

But that Beatles song is often referred to as one of the first recorded instances of feedback. I don't know if that's true – I'm sure there was an occasion in the '50s with a guitarist or some singer. I think those elements are there. I think Zappa and the Mothers were more toward the "proficiency" kind of thing – they also did something edgy – so as far as experimentation, there is certainly stuff going on around the same time as Hendrix, or before. And concurrently there are other people experimenting with these new sounds. He influenced other guitarists to use those elements.

REVEREND HORTON HEAT: Well, he *definitely* brought it to the masses. Yes, there's other guitar players from my perspective. But see, I'm not really a good person to ask. I think that type of question would be better for an average person, because I'm a guitar player – for me, the most groundbreaking thing was the solo on "Rock Around the Clock" in 1954. But that's definitely one thing about him – he brought rock guitar and that sound that really paved the way for Angus Young and all the rock guitar players that came after him. Y'know, they all wanted Marshalls, they all wanted Strats, they all wanted the Fuzz Face pedal.

There is this absolutely unbelievable, great guitar player in Texas, named Rocky Athas. And in the '70s, he had a band called Lightning – in Texas. And he was not only an amazing musician, but his guitar was always perfectly in tune. He was solid with his chords, but his solos were *wild*. They were super-precise, but he did all these tricks – he did the finger-tapping stuff.

And this was *before* Eddie Van Halen. I don't think Eddie Van Halen ever heard of Rocky Athas…I don't know. But when Eddie Van Halen came out and started doing that finger-tapping stuff, Rocky Athas had to quit doing it – because everybody was saying, "Oh, you're just trying to be like Eddie Van Halen." [Laughs] So, that style of guitar playing was out there – that was a thing that was kind of out there.

But Eddie Van Halen broke a lot of ground. I remember when that record came out [1978's *Van Halen*], it was like a bomb going off. I mean, *everybody* got that record. They were like, almost instantly one of the biggest bands in the world. I heard that back in the day, when Van Halen would tour, they had two teams of merchandise sales crews. They couldn't travel with the band, and they had to leapfrog each other, because the crew would sell at the venue one night, and it would take them two days to count the money! And it was consistently over $500,000. So, you think about earning half a million dollars in merch sales at *one gig*. There are still bands that might do that, but back then, $500,000 was kind of like $1,000,000.

RANDY HANSEN: Sure – Robert Johnson. Chet Atkins. Eddie Van Halen. I mean, they didn't change it maybe *as much*, but everyone took it to a new level. You see little kids now that can play "Eruption" – the way that you can learn visually is off the charts. If you want to pick up the guitar, there are so many ways to figure it out. And if you have any rhythm at all, you can get pretty damn good on guitar now.

And if you were to throw that kid who can play "Eruption" now in a time machine, and put him in the days of Jimi Hendrix, people would be bowing down to him. They'd be going, "Jimi's good, but hey, *this kid...*" That's the way it would be. You've got to be the first, that's all. If you're the first, people will be at your door. If you're the second, "*Eh*."

ALEX LIFESON: There certainly have been outstanding and original guitarists who have greatly influenced the direction of rock guitar, and I would cite Eddie Van Halen at the top of that list...just below Jimi Hendrix!

BRUCE KULICK: The only other guy that I feel had an impact and took another generation and really made a huge impression upon a generation – which is still valid – would be Eddie Van Halen. And there were other great players that are influential and important, but for me, I always describe Eddie as an influence for me, too, because he's like the "super-charged car."

 In other words, Hendrix may have been the first Mustang or Ferrari or whatever was around then, but ten years later, Eddie created something that was very powerful on the guitar – incredible technique. And Eddie has always really connected to the instrument and the emotion.

 I hate shredding. I hate a lot of notes in a guitar player. To me, it means nothing and says nothing emotionally. Hendrix was a fast player and Eddie Van Halen a *really* fast player, but they used their speed to move people – and it was never a showboating thing. It was never "take it to an extreme" thing. It was very musical.

 So, I always have a tremendous respect for Eddie...although I think Eddie's biggest influence was Cream-era Eric Clapton and not so much Hendrix. But, add that sense of melody and tone with more speed and a whammy bar – like a Floyd Rose, which gives you the freedom to *really* go wild – and you have a really dangerous player. A guitar player that is really going to change the landscape of lead guitar.

There are the people that love Randy Rhoads, and that was a little different. There are the Yngwie people, the Satriani people – all incredible guitar players, don't get me wrong – but the only other person that I would say that moved me and I know led an entire generation and has continued to is Eddie. I'm positive we'd still be worshipping Hendrix even if he was alive right now. There is no way he would have "pooped" on his career. He might have experimented in things that people didn't understand and he might have not been able to play exactly like the incredible performance that will live forever that we know for the short time that he was on the scene, but he would have carried on.

But it is incredible that when you lose someone that soon and their incredible body of work…it's almost like you can't fault any of it. What are you going to pick on from him? And now of course you can look at Eddie Van Halen's career that went on – it started and stopped, and they did different singers – I always thought Eddie has done quality. But there is that whole controversy of, "Can they get back together with David?" There's always this wanting and discussion and drama.

And it is interesting that those that pass away too young – they're in a time capsule. And the capsule is finite and in a "protective seal," in a sense. But I do feel that Hendrix left us with a body of work that will never be forgotten – and will probably never be surpassed as an innovative guitar player that culturally and musically moved people. He's the top of the tremendous category of guitar players that we love. He's #1 for me.

STEVE VAI: Everybody that plays and contributes is somehow contributing to the change. But every now and then, a *monolith* appears, and it changes the way that the majority of the people may think about the guitar. There's two guitar players that I might point to that perhaps had the biggest influence in the majority of people – Hendrix is one and probably Edward is the other. And my favorite guitar player is Jimmy Page, and I love Page – he was "it" for me.

It's a slippery slope to mention names but Hendrix was a game-changer. And Edward was a game-changer – because he changed many other things about the way we approached rock guitar. The amplifiers we used, the guitars we used, the pickups we used, the whammy bars we used, the sound…it was miraculous.

And there were many other players that were powerful at evolving various aspects of guitar playing. I can point to someone like Allan Holdsworth, and say, "There is nothing like him anywhere on the planet. *Ever*. The end." What he did for the people that are fascinated and connected with that type of playing is as much as what the high school rock n' roll guitar player kid got out of hearing Hendrix. And these are people who I feel found an expression on the instrument that was truly unique. Nothing is *truly* unique…but at least there is an energy and has an independence unlike the others.

I would tell you that Allan is one of them, and

I get that feeling from people like Jimmy Page, Brian May. Brian May was a big one for me – he's so underrated as an evolutionist on the instrument. He was able to blend these unbelievable guitar orchestras into historical pop songs. *Remarkable*. And some other players, like Tommy Emmanuel – he's an acoustic guitar player, and is just a lovely freak. So, there's a lot of players. But I think those two – Edward and Jimi – were "the monoliths."

RON "BUMBLEFOOT" THAL: There have been so many. Eddie Van Halen, for sure. And I've got to say Yngwie Malmsteen. Although you had guys like Uli Jon Roth, and you could even say Ritchie Blackmore – they were planting the seeds of neo-classical hard rock guitar-wise. But Yngwie took it to *such* an extreme, and left a permanent new color wheel of guitar playing. And of course, the greats like Clapton, Vai, and Satch. But the ones that were really 100% modern game-changers were Yngwie, Eddie, and Jimi – ones that made people completely change their gear and change the direction of how they play.

KIRK HAMMETT: When you really think about it, I can say that Eddie Van Halen is "the other Jimi Hendrix" – his contribution to techniques, to sound, to attitude. Even his songwriting is very chordal. Jimi Hendrix and Eddie Van Halen are pretty much in the same circle. But Jimi Hendrix kicks Eddie Van Halen's ass because Jimi did it all in five years! And Eddie has had what, 40 years?

So, I think that's what makes all the

difference in the world, when people say, "Who's the best guitar player?" *Jimi Hendrix is.* And it's not because of just pure technique and who can play faster or whatever. It's what he accomplished in such a short period of time – and how influential it still is to this day. And most importantly, his music begat other types of music.

CASPAR BRÖTZMANN: Sorry, but I don't think so. Jimi Hendrix – "The Blue Wild Angel" – was at the right place at the right time for a short moment of life. Nobody can have this again. The pyramids are there only one time, too.

RICHARD LLOYD: No. Nobody did that. I mean, even all the guitarists in England that are still thought of as the greatest guitarists – like Jimmy Page, Jeff Beck, Pete Townshend – all of them were extremely influenced by Jimi's stage craft. Their jaws all dropped when he first came over, because he was doing things that nobody else had ever done.

Actually, I think Jimi took some of the "hip wiggle" from Pete Townshend. Jimi wasn't afraid to unabashedly borrow something from somebody else – he got a lot from Buddy Guy and Chitlin' Circuit tricks, like swiping the guitar with your elbow and playing it over your head and with your teeth.

But England and America had never seen anything like that. Nobody could ever do it again. Just like nobody could play the guitar with a violin bow, because Jimmy Page did it, and made it his own. So, there's a lot of things that Jimi did that you can't do – that are kind of "off limits." Or else, you're "wearing your Jimi on your sleeve" – in which case,

Jimi is much better at it. I think of him as a rabbit...y'know, at the dog races, they always have a wooden rabbit that goes ahead of the dogs, and the dogs never catch it. I think of him like that – he's my "rabbit." *I'll never catch up to him.*

Chapter 10
Vocalist/Lyricist

Due to his exceptional talent as a guitarist, it's easy to overlook Jimi's singing and lyric-writing.

ALEX LIFESON: He had a great voice that suited his material. Lyrically, the trippy character of his words and thoughts were very cool to a teenage hippie!

STEVE VAI: I loved his singing voice. There was a throwaway nature to the way he sang that really felt organic to him – the way he would throw away certain lines. And his voice had a beautiful register – I liked when he was in that register. From what I understand, he didn't like his singing voice so much – and you can tell, live he would sometimes not be in the mood to even sing very much and not put much into the vocal performance. And then sometimes it was *really* there. His ability to sing worked perfectly with his intentions of the songs.

His lyric-writing was very whimsical in a sense. And there's this perspective of spirituality that is very prominent and was even more prominent in the past – especially in the '60s. And it involved things like metaphysics and particular visuals brought on by drug-induced states of mind. You see it in the artwork – the "acid-y trip" kind of thing. So, whenever you take a substance that alters your mind – especially a psychedelic – it seems as though you're entering some kind of different dimension of reality. And many people believe that that is a spiritual dimension – a *pseudo-spiritual* dimension.

So, when that becomes an alternate sort of reality or perspective, there's a mystique that grows around it. And the mystique that grows involves more psychedelia in things like visuals, clothes that an artist might wear, things they say in the press, the way they write their lyrics, the artwork, the way they present themselves – it's all based on their "mindful perspective," so to speak.

So, I think Jimi's lyric writing, a lot of it came from that. It was quasi-spiritual, whimsical, but incredibly picturesque and imaginative. I mean, "We'll watch the sunrise from the bottom of the sea" – just that one sentence evokes imagination that has a quality to it that doesn't sound trendy or forced. At least to me. And he basically throws the line away. He does it in this relaxed, almost kind of...*haze*. And I just love that. And he was capable of entering that zone and manifesting lyrics.

KIM THAYIL: Some of the lyrics are psychedelic and trippy, and have some profundity to it. Some of the lyrics on *Are You Experienced* are a nice challenge and embrace of wonder – both artistically and soulfully. And some are kind of vapid and pedestrian – I mean, there's not a whole lot to the lyrics of "Fire," really. But then again, "Are You Experienced" is amazing – and "Manic Depression" and "The Wind Cries Mary" are beautiful lyrics.

RICHARD LLOYD: His voice was great – even though he didn't like it. Because, who likes their own voice? Not that many people. Like, John Lennon was always asking to make it sound like he was underwater or through a megaphone or *anything* to change his voice. Jimi was just shy. They had to turn the lights off when he was singing – to get into it. But he got into it live – that's for sure.

RON "BUMBLEFOOT" THAL: I loved it. He was an absolute storyteller. He wasn't someone who was trying to be...there's different types of singers. Bob Dylan could never sing a Pavarotti song, but Pavarotti could never sing a Bob Dylan song. And it's true – everyone has their own voice, and some people are "Broadway," some people are "storytellers." Jimi was absolutely a storyteller – it was like he spoke and gave the lyrics meaning. It's almost a lost art some ways in rock to be a storyteller – we focus so much on technical ability. You think about range, accuracy, pitch, and vibrato and all that stuff is fine, but sometimes, just saying what the words mean get lost. Jimi didn't do that.

He had *some* range – he could hit some high notes. He didn't do it often – just like he wouldn't do a quick speed run on the guitar. But every so often he would reach up and hit something that's a bit up there. Not "old school metal" up there, but just top of the range. It was almost like he sang the way he spoke, in a way. The way the notes would bend. Like, he wouldn't go, "*AHHHHH*!" He'd go, "*Hey*!" And he wasn't trying to be dead-on the beat – he was phrasing the way people speak would say it. He definitely emphasized the message of the lyrics.

And no way was he a bad singer – he was actually a great singer. He was very influential in that aspect, as well. But the fact that he was being who he is – he wasn't trying to sing like someone other than himself. There are a lot of singers that are trying to be the type of singers they want to be – not the singer they are. He had authenticity – he was *very* genuine.

RIK EMMETT: He wasn't a great singer, but he sort of figured out that it's not necessarily about...he loved Dylan, and no one would say Dylan was an unbelievably great singer, either. But as a vocalist, it's an incredible style. Here in Canada, they have the Junos – which are the Grammys – and one year, Leonard Cohen won "male vocalist of the year." To which – in his extremely dry wit – he said, "Well, of course. *That's because of my golden voice.*" [Laughs] He's not much of a singer, either, but he's a stylist. So, Hendrix had figured that out as a singer. And it's a really unique, really great singing voice – even though he didn't like his own voice.

Triumph made an album with Eddie Kramer [1984's *Thunder Seven*], and Eddie said, "Jimi hated the sound of his own voice." He also hated anybody seeing him, so they'd build a little hut on the studio floor of gobos [isolation panels], so that you couldn't see him. And he would be inside this little sheltered space, and he would do his vocals that way – because he didn't want anybody watching him sing.

That's an interesting thing – that there was a war going on inside him, about being a pop kind of person. And I think sometimes those kinds of things help fuel the individualism or the unique qualities of what actually ends up coming out. And that would be true of everything with Jimi – his guitar playing, his singing, his striving for something that would be stylistically unique.

BRUCE KULICK: I loved his voice. I thought it

was R&B-oriented. He "talk-sang" in a way sometimes – which there is nothing wrong with that. I thought it was perfect – I really did. And I'm glad he did it. I don't think he was comfortable with it – from what I understand. I think I used to read things about him being a bit uncomfortable being the singer, but I still think all that swagger and attitude would shine better from him presenting himself as a singer. So, I welcomed it.

And he was a very creative lyricist. Back then, people were taking a lot of drugs, too, so it was pretty easy to get out there about your references. But I think he was prolific – his lyrics and how he played with sexual topics to talk about the inner mind or the inner soul, all that stuff. And he was rebellious – "If 6 Was 9," where he doesn't want to be "establishment." I think he was a great, great songwriter. Really terrific.

REVEREND HORTON HEAT: Well, I think as a singer, he was one of these guys that was a hot guitar player – which is kind of similar to my deal. I mean, I wasn't a hot guitar player, but I was a lead guitar player in bands with other singers and I didn't sing. So, when I started getting my own original music together, I had to start singing.

And I've heard from a lot of people that Jimi Hendrix did not like to hear himself sing. He did not like his voice. He was very shy about his voice. But y'know man, it was great – it was bluesy. He had an authentic-sounding bluesy voice. "Castles Made of Sand" is awesome singing.

CURT KIRKWOOD: He was a great singer.

Perfect. Again, when you hear Jimi Hendrix sing…*it's Jimi Hendrix*. Nobody else sounds like that. The idiosyncrasy – something makes it different. It's not cookie cutter.

EAST BAY RAY: He's not the best singer in rock music, but a combination of his guitar...and the bass player and drummer – Noel Redding and Mitch Mitchell – there's this chemistry that happens in bands. There's a mysterious side that you can't really plan, but it happens sometimes. And when it happens, it just makes everybody play better, and *you* play better. And I think that happened with them. I can't imagine the records with another singer.

With guitar players, I would rather hear one note from Muddy Waters than 32 32nd notes from some shredder. And the same thing with the voice. There are feelings from people who can sing, feelings from playing guitar. But to get that soul and that communication into it, and then having another person respond to it is a different level. I mean, I like Howlin' Wolf's singing...but how would you classify *his* voice?

RANDY HANSEN: A song like "Axis: Bold as Love" – just the way he delivers it and it shows his Dylan influence, and his psychedelic mind in the lyrics. The lyrics in that song are great. It's *so* poetic. His poetry is wonderful. He was a great singer – I love his voice. He has a great voice. I've aspired to sing like him – among other people. But Jimi's voice, it was a voice of God. I would say he came the closest.

"1983" definitely [contains some of Randy's

favorite lyrics that Jimi penned]. I like his songs that warn people of the future. I think those are the most important ones, because who knows how far down the line he was...or maybe Jimi was just a psychedelic guy and took a lot of acid? You never know.

Somehow, the guy seemed to have insight. I don't know where it came from. But I'm always open to either story – I just try and keep my mind open. I had a lot of wild things happen to me that make me believe in an afterlife. I won't bore you with it but they were life-changing things that happened to me that pointed to that. Everyone has their beliefs – but I think we should all keep them personal.

RON "BUMBLEFOOT" THAL: Loved it. Poetic. How the hell did he come up with the things he came up with? "The Wind Cries Mary," let's say. I just did a cover of that at the Jakarta Blues Festival. I was memorizing the words – because I'm terrible at memorizing the lyrics – and just reading them a hundred times, and thinking, "Where did he get this poetry?" I mean, "Traffic lights they turn blue tomorrow" – there's a simplicity that makes you picture something that you wouldn't have otherwise pictured.

And I think that influenced me, too. "Somewhere a queen is weeping, Somewhere a king has no wife." I have a song on my last album [2015's *Little Brother Is Watching*], "Cuterebra," and somewhere in there I do the same queen and king thing – "'Neath the card house all my kings are buried and the queen won't say a word." He was a fantastic lyricist. Extremely poetic without being sappy or cheesy. It was just imaginative. His lyrics were visionary.

RIK EMMETT: The tragedy of Hendrix dying at 27 is that you don't get the maturation of a guy moving into his thirties and forties, and hearing what that does to him as a songwriter. So, early Hendrix – the stuff that we got – it's poetic. He clearly had a really lovely gift. And again with what I was saying about his visualization and imagery – which was really good. It was *vivid*.

But on the downside of it, it's kind of like, I hear it as it's like a young guy doing a young guy's take on culture. I don't think he was necessarily rising to the level of a Bob Dylan yet. Did he have the potential to be a Bob Dylan lyricist? Yes. I believe that. Which is part of the tragedy – we didn't get to see it.

He was very much a blues kind of guy. He was very much an improvising…kind of, "Let's smoke some dope, let's drop some acid, and let's play." Which is not like somebody who goes, "OK, I'm going to lock myself up in a cabin and cleanse my body with only the right foods, and I'm going to spend four months just writing. It's going to be me, my pencil, and my notebook."

And because the culture was so wide open – both as a writer and as a player – Hendrix tended to be…there was kind of a lack of discipline in what was going on there. Yes, there was a tremendous gift, but also, this kind of hippie, kind of lack of discipline…I would have been happier if he got to live longer.

Like, there is a story – I don't know if it's apocryphal or not – where Miles Davis invited

Hendrix over and was thinking about doing some kind of a project with him. They were at dinner or something, and then Miles said something or put some charts in front of Jimi or talked about playing in modes or something like that.

And Jimi said, "Well...I can't read music. I don't know what you're talking about." To which Miles kind of scoffed, and said, "Well, *that's that*," and kind of wiped his hands of Jimi Hendrix. I don't know if it's a true story or not, but it is illustrative of a fact that there's a side to being a musician, which requires a certain amount of discipline, which Hendrix didn't really have.

KIRK HAMMETT: Before this interview, I was thinking that I know Jimi asked Miles Davis to play in the studio with him. And Miles Davis demanded 50 grand [according to the 1991 book, *Crosstown Traffic: Jimi Hendrix & The Post-War Rock n' Roll Revolution*, by Charles Shaar Murray]. And 50 grand back in the late '60s/early '70s…that was like *half a million dollars* in today's money.

RIK EMMETT: But if he'd had more life, if he'd lived longer, he might have become somebody who at some point would have said, "I've got to learn modes. I've got to do this. I can't do it all by ear." And then probably would have been somebody who said, "I've got to go to school or whatever made Bob Dylan the kind of songwriter that Bob Dylan is. I need to dive deep into that." You look at Hendrix's life, and he spent time in the military, he was traveling around, he was a sideman...Dylan didn't do any of that stuff. Dylan was just woodshedding on

"I'm going to be a folk singer. I'm going to be a writer. And I'm going to write like all these other folk guys writing."

And a lot of Dylan songs are based on old folk song forms. Like, he was borrowing *heavily* in his early stages. And so was Jimi. Jimi was borrowing heavily as a blues guy. And at 27, I'm not sure you've necessarily fully come into your own – in terms of depth and discipline. I've always felt that way about Hendrix, that's the real tragedy for me – the world was cheated of somebody who I think had the talent and the ability and the imagination to be able to embrace the discipline as time went on.

Chapter 11
Equipment & Techniques

*Which guitar and studio equipment/techniques is
Jimi most associated with?*

RON "BUMBLEFOOT" THAL: I would say
Electro-Harmonix pedals…and lighter fluid.
[Laughs] And left-handed guitars. But to me, those
two things come to mind – Electro-Harmonix pedals
and playing left-handed…or right-handed but just
flipped over. Electro-Harmonix pedals were cutting
edge technology. At that point, the guitar was at the
forefront of modern sound. And Jimi Hendrix was
taking it to the next level. He was pioneering new
sounds that ears had never heard before.

I mean, I remember as a kid when I was
taking guitar lessons at this music store, and because
of Jimi I remember getting a Big Muff. He was the
one that was pushing…I don't know pushing the
limits, but *raising the bar* of guitar technology. You
could say that of Electro-Harmonix, but Jimi wasn't
the one looking the other way at some of the whacky
things you could do when you have feedback and
you're turning the nob and making it twist and
creating all these strange sounds.

It was the combination – you had a company
like Electro-Harmonix that was making some really
unique pedals and you had Jimi that took it under his
wing – no pun intended – and started really using the
stuff in his sound. And again, capturing those
moments, where something different can happen
every night if you turn the nob of a Memory Man and
it starts to feedback within itself and you have it crash

down.

He was making *sounds* – between the two of them, the marriage of Electro-Harmonix and Jimi Hendrix. They were bringing sounds to people's ears that were never being heard before in all of mankind. It was *very* special. I think today, anything that's already been done, people don't realize what it's like to hear it for the first time. I mean, it was a *huge* impact and it just changed guitar.

BRUCE KULICK: Number one would be the wah wah pedal. The other one would be distortion. The overdrive pedals he used – like Fuzz Face and stuff like that – they worked really well with the cleaner, loud Marshalls and a Strat. I don't particularly care for what they do for my sound – with a Marshall amp that has more gain in it. But that was an essential part of his sound.

The Univibe is the other one. I have an original Univibe like Hendrix's, and they've gone up in value like crazy. Of course, there are a million companies that make versions of them – some of them quite good, actually. He had his tech guy that knew how to build things make him an Octavia pedal – that had a special sound to it.

RANDY HANSEN: I think Eric Clapton was the one that gave Jimi the idea to do that [to use guitar effects]. But Jimi was actually using a Fuzztone back then at the same time – before he ever heard Eric. It just wasn't a good one – it was that Maestro Fuzz…and the band hated it. [Laughs] But I think there were others…like "Spirit in the Sky," there was a fuzz box around before Jimi used it. It's just that's what happened when he used it.

And he was into Buck Rogers and science fiction movies – I think that's why he made so many sounds, rather than just playing notes. A lot of times, it was all about sound. And thank God – because the balance that he got, I'm sure he was at times just as surprised as anyone with what was coming out.

It's really close now [Randy's set-up compared to Jimi's]. I'm playing through all-black Celestions. I'm playing through only the bottom cabinets – a lot of people don't know that Jimi didn't really hook up the top cabs. He liked the way it looked – the same as me. They're a little loud when you do that, and I'd be deaf today if I didn't do that. Now, I've got ahold of a vintage Marshall Major – there's a chance it's the Marshall Major that Ritchie Blackmore threw off the stage at Cal Jam [in 1974]. It sounds wonderful. And I use that to daisy chain off to a couple more Marshalls.

I'm basically using the exact set-up as Jimi – Fuzz Face, Vox Wah, Echoplex sometimes, Octavia, Univibe. I don't particularly like to tell the order – just because it took me a while to arise at what is correct, and I don't like to just throw that out there. It was fun for me to go on a journey of discovery – to try and discover, "How is he making these sounds and make them sound right?" And that's what I've been all about as far as Jimi.

ADRIAN BELEW: In his live show, Jimi didn't actually have the opportunity to use that many effects. They didn't exist yet! Les Paul was the father of electric guitar, Jimi was the father of guitar effects. Just imagine the huge industry that exists because of what he started. But back then, a Fuzzbox, a Wah Wah, a Univibe, a giant stack of amps: those were his basic tools. So, for me it was his use of studio effects on his records (helped along with his engineer/ producer Eddie Kramer) that was utterly ground-breaking.

The backwards guitar in the song "Are You Experienced" – mind-blowing. Backwards guitar is another Hendrix trademark I've used so many times. The sound of stereo flanging especially on *Axis: Bold As Love* and *Electric Ladyland* just turned the entire sound of those records inside out – along with all the radical panning.

It seemed like every other song had a different guitar sound no one had used before. He was incredibly versatile of course with just his Stratocaster through an amp – he could pull more sounds out of it than anyone, but the main thing was his mastery of effects: delays, fuzz tones, tape manipulations, feedback, chorusing, flanging; all new weapons at the time. The effect on me personally was electric (excuse the pun!).

I was just starting to teach myself how to play acoustic guitar – just to write songs – when, "Wow, listen to what you can do with an electric guitar!" Hendrix, Beck, Clapton. It fired up my imagination, made me want to be more than a songwriter – it dragged me into the waiting universe of playing lead electric guitar. It was so inspiring that I listened and learned something every day. It became my life 24/7.

ANDY POWELL: I would use the tremolo on a guitar in a very delicate way – it's always been part of my technique, just to give it a shimmer to the sound. But Jimi was taking it into "psychedelic" – he was doing divebombs, jet planes, and all kinds of stuff. So, I think he was the guy that *really* opened up everyone's eyes and minds and ears to the sonic possibilities with the guitar. And it was a Fender Strat, as well – which is a difficult guitar to do that stuff on, because you've got single coil pickups, and things squealing all over the place.

And of course, he tapped into the Marshall amps – we were all using these big, heavy English amps at the time. I was using Laney. I opened for the Who for a couple of shows, and I saw the stacks coming out, and we saw these 4x12's. And of course, Jimi tapped right into that and that became part of his sound, as well. And I think the combination, and very specifically, moving to London, and the fashion, using these giant stacks that were feeding back and howling all over the place – that's really what he was feeding off of. Those elements were creating sound.

So, it's kind of synergy – it was the perfect place for him to be. And the development of all those amps at that time. If you think back to America at the time, a Marshall Plexi 50-watt amp took the design of a Fender Bassman – I have a '59 Bassman and still use it in the studio – but he took that, and just copied that design, and hooked it up to a 4x12 cabinet with Celestion speakers.

That was another important component – Celestions with the amp heads. And then, of course we got 100-watt heads. Trying to control a beast like that on stage…even now, I've got a nice old 100-watt Marshall, and I sometimes bring it out on the road. It's a bloody *loud* amplifier – as are the Orange 100's.

I used to use two of those on stage, and at one point, I was using two 200-watt Orange amp heads. Now, that is a clean hi-fi-sounding guitar amp – with tons of headroom and cartridge transformers. These amps were *so* loud, but in a way, they had to be. If you think back in the time, we were doing stadiums – as was Jimi – and the PA's were puny. So, you needed to project the guitar sound from the stage. And I think he really picked up on that – and he could fill an auditorium with Marshall amplification. And it was dynamic.

And the same thing for us – when we came to the States, we were using Orange, and the soundguys had never heard anything like it. We packed the 4x12's with actually American speakers – JBL K-120's – and the Orange heads at 200-watts each. You actually didn't need a PA! I think all that went into sound.

RANDY HANSEN: There is a trick to that [keeping a non-locking Strat in tune while using the tremolo bar]. One, you want to keep the nut on that really nice and greased up. You can put any kind of oil on there. You can take grease off your nose and put it on there – if you've got nothing else. Another thing, take the G string out from underneath the string tree that's on the headstock. And then, while you're tuning, each note as you tune it, the last thing you should do is hit the vibrato bar, and then look at the tuner and see if the note isn't now still in tune.

If it's not, then account for it by you really have to stretch the strings good, and then usually when you hit the bar, the note will have a tendency to go sharp, because what's happening is the string is traveling through the nut, and then you're letting the bar loose, and it's not coming back all the way. But the same tension on the springs is there, so it's going sharp. So, what you want to do is you want to make sure that the vibrato bar is what keeps the guitar in tune. This is how I play, and I'm pretty sure this is what Jimi did too, and this is why people went, "Wow. How can he hit the bar so much?"

If you end up using the bar, it helps keep the guitar in tune. In other words, every time you hit it, you look at the tuner and you see now if it's in tune. Now, when you go out there in front of the people and you're playing, you'll bend a note, and as soon as you bend that note, the guitar is out of tune – because you've pulled the strings through too far. Now, the tension is going to be different on it. But now, what you do in order to get back in tune – you hit the bar, and it brings it back. *That's the way.*

CASPAR BRÖTZMANN: The difference [between Caspar's guitar set-up and Jimi's] is my Boss chorus effect pedal and the old Rat distortion with a bigger black box and the filter is different to the new Rats. I also use a Vox wah wah. In times of Massaker, I played the usual 100-watt Super Lead Marshall amps like Page, Blackmore, Hendrix, and all the other thousands of guitar players, too.

I am sorry, you don't need me for any tips or advice [concerning controlling feedback while soloing]. You need a room or better stage and turn on your amps and play like hell, and do this for years, and then you will know exactly how to call and catch feedbacks you are looking for. Maybe once in advice, you must find out how it feels to go over your limits.

If you are playing over three Marshall stacks, this is a really heavy experience without earplugs. And this high volume pumps you up full of energy, and you will be riding in a storm through walls of sounds. And after the show when the first push is gone, you are completely empty.

Do this for maybe two hours and then you can feel how it was in the late-60's/early-70's to stand on stage with just a simple PA system in front of 400,000 people – for example. In other words, the backline by these times was different from what we know today – like a big PA system left and right from stage. I think that this "wall of sound" pushes Hendrix's playing a lot.

EAST BAY RAY: I don't think he ever did [use an Echoplex – an effect that became Ray's trademark]. But I know they used effects on the records – recording studio effects. Not echo so much, but I do remember listening to some songs where they do panning back and forth. But the thing I liked about Jimi Hendrix was how much he was outside the box – in the sense that he played with Little Richard and King Curtis.

That's kind of cool – it's kind of similar to John Coltrane in a sense that they learned the rules really, really well, so they knew how to break them...on purpose, not by accident. I think if you don't do that, it's hard to get outside the box – unless you know what the box is. And he had hits on the radio. And personally, I like Hendrix's melodic stuff.

Jimi had a Uni-Vibe Phase Shifter, and I was able to get one for $20 from somebody – back in the late '70s. And I actually used it on some of our recordings – I didn't use it live, but I used it on some of our recordings. It's one of my prized possessions, because it's a very whacky device, and very rare. I used it pretty subtly, because it's a very radical effect, and it didn't really quite fit Dead Kennedys. More than likely, it would have been something off *Plastic Surgery Disasters* and *Frankenchrist*. There's a lot of things on records that you don't notice, but if you took it away, you'd go, "Oh...*something's missing.*" It wasn't to the level that he used it – which was pretty radical.

CHEETAH CHROME: The fuzz box...it was a Fuzz Face, and I thought, "I've got to try one of those." It was a fun tool. But Hendrix, he made it sound like a wah wah through *his fingers*. There was something more personal in Hendrix than most people when they write.

BRIAN TATLER: I don't have anything that Jimi used. I think he used a Fuzz Face, and I don't know what wah wah – it might have been a Jim Dunlop. I haven't gotten into his effects or amplifiers to that degree. When I was learning to play, I had moved on to other guitarists, like Schenker, Blackmore, Page, and then, Van Halen. I didn't want to copy Hendrix. I didn't want to sound like Hendrix. I think he has influenced every guitarist that has come since, but by the time I started learning – when I was 15 in 1975 – I had moved on to other players. So, I was studying people like Ritchie Blackmore and Michael Schenker.

ANDY POWELL: I thought Jimi was so perfectly

aligned with the Stratocaster that I thought it was a mismatch [when Jimi would play a Gibson Flying V – a make/model that Andy has become synonymous with]. Although, visually, of course it looked dynamic. But no, I never paid attention to him playing that. I don't even think I was aware of that actually until later – when I saw some pictures of him. My experience with him was solely using the Strat.

In fact, it was so impressive to me that I used to build guitars, and the Stratocaster was such a sexy-looking sculptural thing, that the first guitar I ever built – at age 15 – was a Fender Strat-style guitar. And he would have made a big impression on me. But it was only later that I saw pictures of him using a V – I didn't think it really worked with his style at all. If I'm totally honest, I'd say my use of the V was for more in tune with what my personal intrinsic style was. He's a Strat player through and through – I think most people would agree with that.

CURT KIRKWOOD: Oh, I'd think the Strat is probably "his instrument." There are clips of him playing acoustic stuff – but it's still Jimi. I think no matter what he played, it would have been that. He wasn't afraid of "the raw." I started out on Les Pauls because I thought they looked cool! [Laughs] I played it so much – but once I started playing a Strat, it's a different thing. *Huevos* is all my '65 Telecaster – but that's a chunkier guitar than a Strat. It's just not as raw. I would imagine just about anything would have been fair game in his hands. It's coming from *the dude* – not ultimately the instrument. Like I said, you hear him playing an acoustic guitar, and it's like,

"Yep. That's Jimi Hendrix."

ALEX LIFESON: The Uni-Vibe, wah wah pedal…and finger picking.

MICHAEL SCHENKER: I don't even remember anything that Jimi Hendrix did on the wah wah pedal. If I remember anything from Jimi Hendrix and the wah wah pedal, it just went, "Wah, wah, wah, wah, wah." I don't think he did anything else. What I did with the wah wah pedal was I discovered that there was a sweet spot in the EQ, and I wanted to find out how I was able to find the position to keep that sweet spot in an instant.

So, I had a look inside the wah wah pedal to see how it works. It looked very simple, so I just positioned that wheel – that thing that grabbed the wheel – into the position, by putting it down. I first found the note, and then put it in a position of when that sound was available in the down position. So, I only had to press the wah wah pedal, and then I had the instant sweet spot.

Which, by the way, there was one song that I rediscovered, "Lookin' Out for No. 1" [off UFO's *Obsession*] – which was written by Paul Raymond – and I made an instrumental out of it, and it was called "Lookin' Out for No. 1 (Reprise)," and that was playing with a wah wah pedal. And it sounds incredible. I didn't know it sounded that good. It was just one position – just the sweet spot – and it's a perfect example of what I did with it.

Also, I did it on "Alone Again Or" [off UFO's *Lights Out*]. It's a song by Love, that had a saxophone solo on the original version, and I did the same thing there – I played that saxophone, but I played it with a wah wah pedal in the sweet spot position, and it sounds fantastic. That was the kind of stuff I did.

But the wah wah pedals became worse and worse. The components went thinner and thinner. They were breaking down, and with the components, no new ones were made – and the wah wah pedals became worse. At that point, I kept old wah wah pedals for so long, that the guitar sound became so thin – it was ridiculous. It was stupid. I didn't even notice it. So, my guitar sound started to suffer at some point when I carried on playing on the wah wah pedal, when I shouldn't have – because it was actually turning into a junk sound. It was getting really bad.

If you compare the original sweet spot sound with a later version of the run-down and broke wah wah pedal, you can hear the difference. And then when you have something great that works great and the components wind up not being made anymore, you lose it. So, I'm glad that I found the JCM800 [an amplifier by Marshall]. And of course, they have run out of components – they can't even make the JCM800 anymore. But wah wah-wise, I hear something in my head that just goes "Wah, wah, wah, wah" – when Jimi Hendrix played wah wah. That's the only thing I think that he did.

KIRK HAMMETT: He was the master of that 7 sharp 9 chord. It's in *so many* of the songs. It's known as "the Hendrix chord." It's funny because in that Junior Walker song, "Shotgun," *that's* the chord! That chord is super, super important. I learned how to finger that chord three or four different ways – from Stevie Ray Vaughan. There are at least three different ways to finger that chord – and each way, it's so cool and so effective.

FRANK MARINO: There were *two* Jimi Hendrixes in the world – according to the listener. There was the Jimi Hendrix of the production of Chas Chandler…which is the one we all know – the first two albums and part of the third, because some of those songs were supposed to be on *Axis*. And then there's the stuff after Jimi died – *Cry of Love*, which wasn't finished.

But then then there's the stuff afterwards that Alan Douglas gave to the world, which is the live Marshall/Stratocaster Jimi Hendrix playing blues-based rock. Jamming. That's a completely different Jimi Hendrix than the first two albums. It's a totally different guy. And most of the "Hendrix disciples" of today take their cue from the later stuff. That's what they copy. They very rarely – if ever – go into the psychedelic purity of *Are You Experienced*, *Axis: Bold as Love*, and *Electric Ladyland*. That's the *other* Jimi Hendrix.

As far as I'm concerned, that's the Jimi Hendrix for me. I might like a little bit of Band of Gypsys because it's pretty reasonably well-recorded and there are a couple of great tunes on it. But that's not the Jimi Hendrix I know. So, if I'm going to cover Jimi Hendrix, I'm going to cover Jimi Hendrix from that era. And I'm going to try to be true to that sound – not just say that I'm going to play guitar solos as a cover of Jimi Hendrix.

Because he's not a guitar soloist – he's a

"sound guy." He's painting a picture. And you can take all of the "Blue Suede Shoes" and rock n' roll tunes you want of Jimi doing that stuff...but I know what it is to go out and do a gig and fill up the time with an hour and play whatever you want. But it's not the same when you sit down and get creative.

And by the way, just to tell you, I think Chas Chandler doesn't get enough credit. If you actually look at the influence of Chandler's production with Jimi Hendrix on the first two albums and part of the third one, we *really* see a marked difference when he lets Chandler go and he produces it himself.

Because on *Electric Ladyland*, you have tunes that quite obviously had the Chandler influence – such as "All Along the Watchtower," "Crosstown Traffic," and stuff like that. You can see the influence. But then you have Jimi doing his "jam tunes" – whether it's "Still Raining, Still Dreaming," "Rainy Day, Dream Away," "1983," "Voodoo Chile" – it's kind of two different things.

You wouldn't expect to see those tracks on *Axis* or *Are You Experienced*. Nor would you see the earlier tracks from *Experienced* or *Axis* on *Electric Ladyland*. I see a split there, and you really see the difference between Chandler being not involved or having been involved. I don't know what Hendrix's relationship was like with Chandler – if they didn't get along or he didn't like what he did. I have no idea why he stopped using him at all.

BRUCE KULICK: Obviously, Eddie Kramer was important – since he had the knowledge of a recording studio...and I don't think that Hendrix as an artist grew up in a recording studio. He was just so innovative with the instrument and what he heard in his head. I think Eddie's role was probably very much interpreting and being the "hands on the equipment" to help him do the panning, the ping-ponging, the flanging, the mic techniques, the reverbs, the ambient sounds of certain songs.

I think it was a wonderful experience that Eddie was blessed to have. And I certainly have the utmost respect for him as an engineer – to have had that opportunity [to work with Eddie when Bruce was a member of Kiss]. He was instrumental in letting Hendrix being the icon that he became.

In that short period of time that Jimi was prolific, it's incredible how much he came up with. And then who knows if it was just Eddie Kramer fulfilling Jimi's wishes, like, "I want it to sound like *this*. How can we do that?" Just like the way that the Beatles used to push the engineers at the BBC, who were trained that way at EMI – "No, it has to be *brighter*." Hendrix was challenging Eddie Kramer, and they were doing some incredible things in the studio.

There are so many innovative effects that Jimi created and was instrumental in sharing – and they're still valid and still really important in rock guitar. It's just mind-blowing.

RIK EMMETT: Hendrix...we haven't even touched on record production. He made huge leaps in that sense, that he would go, "No, no, no. Hey Eddie, mix those things down, so we can free up some more tracks." See, Hendrix was happening right at that time where there was the explosion of more tracks – and the ability to mix down to open up more tracks, so you can add more stuff, or you can do another thing, or do something on another day.

Electric Ladyland was mind-blowing in terms of studio production qualities that existed on that record. There had not been an album like that. And Jimi was doing it out of creativity. Like, when the Beatles were expanding in that sense, in terms of record production, they had George Martin there with them, and all these EMI engineers in white coats. So, there is probably a more pristine thing to it – when it was the Beatles with EMI.

But in Jimi's case, it was just Jimi forcing engineers to try things and do things, and say, "No, no, no. I need to make it sound like it's *underwater*. We've got to get some kind of flanging wobble." So, there would be these things that would happen – that he would make them do things where the engineers would say, "Well, I've never done that before, because that seems to kind of be breaking the rules. But OK Jimi, we'll give it a shot." That was another sort of "pioneering quality" to the guy as a recording artist. He was pushing the envelope in that sense.

Chapter 12
Today's Technology

What would Jimi have done with today's gadgets?

STEVE VAI: That is a good question and there is a lot of speculation on it. Some people believe that he died at the perfect time – he left a beautiful-looking corpse. A 27-year-old corpse. And didn't have to confront keeping up with his himself, so to speak. Because it's not uncommon that an artist peaks at that point, and everything after that is more or less within of the vein of what they're doing with little kind of creative off-shoots that expand their vision a little bit here and there. And sometimes, there's a curve where they just go down and they're not capable of really embracing that kind of creativity on a one-up level each time they do something.

Also, some greatly creative people can get involved in things that cut at the root at their creativity – such as financial disaster, relationship disaster, getting involved in drugs. And then there are those kinds of artists that are continually raising their bar – not for any other reason but they enjoy it. There may be pressure from the outside world to continue to evolve, but that's not usually the reason why truly creative, evolutionary artists evolve.

They evolve because that's their tension – they're not satisfied repeating themselves. Frank Zappa was like that. And there are other artists – like David Bowie. And I just discovered not too long ago this band, Ghost. That guy, Tobias Forge, I think he's a complete genius and he's never going to be happy resting on his laurels, so to speak.

Now, what would Jimi Hendrix have done? No one can say. My instincts tell me if I were to rely on them – and they don't mean anything at this point – that Hendrix would have *soared*. He would have continued to explore things in ways that would guide us all – on a particular level. When it comes to production, when it comes to digital and the way that I've seen the ability of the industry to evolve technologically on the side of guitars and guitar effects and guitar amplifiers. I might assume that he would have really explored all that stuff and be at the forefront on the development of things that we maybe don't even have right now.

I can't say how his state of mind would have developed – and that's always joined at the hip at what you manifest into the world. Your state of mind is the foundation of what you manifest. So, really, what his state of mind would have been? Who knows?

BILLY SHEEHAN: Through the timeline, I think he would have probably peaked out on that stuff during the mid-late '70s and probably would have gone another way. That's just my feeling on it. And with an acoustic guitar or a straight-up Strat through a Fender Twin Reverb or a Marshall – I think. Because I see a lot of guys that went through that whole "effects/technology thing" started to grow, and I know a lot of guys who *didn't* grow with it – they touched on it initially and they were the pioneers of it, but then they backed off from it. So, I don't know if Jimi would have gotten heavily into that kind of thing.

His forefront/most important talent was

blues-like screaming rock and his voice and songwriting. And I don't think you can really do much to that technologically to enhance it – because I don't want to hear anything else other than Jimi's voice and guitar with a band. Playing swirling synthesizer things and an endless amount of pedalboards, I'm not sure if that would have helped much. But that's wishful thinking, too – who knows? Maybe he would have gone completely off the deep end and quit guitar and played theremin, and we would have never heard from him again!

RON "BUMBLEFOOT" THAL: *Oooo!* He hopefully wouldn't have lost his innovative spirit, and his curiosity and passion for creativity. It's easy for people to burn out and become complacent. It can happen to everyone. I would hope that he would have embraced things like guitar synths. And who knows what could have been? People always wonder, "What would he have been doing if he never died?" A lot of people guess he would be playing fusion and it would be some very unusual guitar sounds – beyond just a regular guitar. I bet he would have loved the fretless.

KIRK HAMMETT: He was an innovator. He was the type of innovator that anything you put in his hands, he would have taken it and innovated it. He was like…*a painter with sound.* And so, if you think about all the technology, all the different sort of things that created sound that has come in the wake of the time period between now and when he died – that's *a lot* of stuff.

　　You have synthesizers, the first wave of

modern guitar effects which happened in the '70s – which, was really inspired by Jimi, because he was the first major "effects guy." I'm sure he would have been on top of all the new sounds that came out.

And a lot of those effects pedals came out so that it would be convenient to get a sound that was similar to what Jimi's sound was in the studio. What he was doing in the studio was a direct influence on what MXR was doing, Electro-Harmonix was doing – all those early effects companies...Ibanez, Maxon. They were just trying to figure out how to get the phasing and the flanging that's all throughout *Axis* and *Electric Ladyland.*

There were guys that were hearing that and going, "We need to figure out how he got that...*and put it in a box!*" And then all of a sudden, what shows up? Electro-Harmonix comes up with this sort of weird flange-phase thing...or was it Univox? I can't remember – the first person that came up with a phase shifting sort of vibe. But I believe it was because of the sound that Jimi Hendrix was getting in the studio.

So, having said all that – he would have been a sound innovator – for sure. And with sampling? Oh man! I see Jimi Hendrix's later career as being similar to Miles Davis' – where he works with current musical trends, while keeping another foot in tradition. And that's what Miles did – a lot – and did other genres of music while doing that. I believe that Jimi would have discovered – or opened up – other possibilities to other types of music. Who knows? He might have discovered earlier a lot of what we eventually did discover...or maybe there is something that we still haven't discovered, that we would have discovered if Jimi was around. He was *that* innovative.

ANDY POWELL: Guitar technology has really come a long way since then – he was always re-tuning the guitar on stage. And he brought it into the act – because the guitar was always going out of tune. Very hard to use these light gauge strings he was using – these slinky strings, with a banjo string on the top E, and then doing his divebomb stuff with the tremolo. No one had heard anyone do that stuff. And he would just take the guitar and rip the hell out of it. And of course, the problem was at the end of a song, there would be a massive amount of time re-tuning. But he would turn that into part of the act, as well.

BRUCE KULICK: I just think he wouldn't have had to tune on stage as much in between songs. What he was doing on a regular floating tremolo of a Stratocaster is exactly what a Floyd Rose does – except a Floyd Rose…it's not fair to say it does it better, it just does it more efficiently. Because obviously by having something locking – the chances of the strings slipping and going out of tune during a performance have gone down.

Now, Eddie Van Halen *really* introduced it. I think Hendrix would have been just a little more efficient – but I don't think he would have changed much. And maybe he still would have preferred a Strat. The Strat evolved a little bit – where Jeff Beck never uses a Floyd Rose, he uses a regular Strat but he has a roller nut, which helps so the guitar won't go out of tune when he does some of his whammy stuff. So, there are ways that players have improved upon it.

He was a pioneer, Jimi. Those guitars weren't straight out of the box from Manny's – he did have people tinker on it and improve them. There were pedals that were created for him. He was always experimenting – him and Eddie Kramer and the things they did in the studio. But you've got to remember, even on a primitive level – meaning he's one of the guys to introduce, innovate, and start some of these things, including using a Stratocaster tremolo system not in any way that anyone else did originally – he was just a fabulous innovator of all those things. We have so much that we owe to him.

ADRIAN BELEW: Sometimes I wonder, "What would Jimi be doing now? What would the 'mature artist Jimi Hendrix' be writing and singing? What would have he made of guitar synthesizers? Or sampling? Or the myriad of effects available now which would have no doubt excited his imagination?" In a sense, he gifted that to the world – the interest that guitar players have had ever since and cool sounds and different styles and pedals and the variety of guitars and amps, has to go back to him. He's the father of it.

KIM THAYIL: Because he came to not avert his ears from the emotive nature of his playing...or the soulful nature of his playing, he seemed to initiate and pursue experimentation. He wasn't afraid to use elements of chaos and improvisation. I disagree with the studio rats who think that somehow he embraced "clean" and the effects that would augment the proficient nature of his playing.

Maybe he would have done a record that was like fusion – it's very likely. And he probably would have done something proggy. But I doubt that he would have strayed too far from his emotive and soulful nature as a player. I'm sure he would have continued that – that sort of volatile aspect of his personality, and would come through in his playing.

This is the guy who humped his amp, smashed his guitar, and set it on fire! Why do the studio rats think he would polish his guitar and wipe the control board clean? People – I think correctly – embrace him as being a guy of love and peace, and yet these other people say, "No! He wasn't that. He was all about the strength and he was powerful" – like he was Zeus or Thor or something. [Laughs]

There's varied understandings of people's body of work and what they have imparted. It may be a tough call of Hendrix…but I doubt that he would have become a studio rat – in terms of proficiency. I think he would have experimented with effects to augment to how he could express himself – but not necessarily to augment a technique or proficiency.

REVEREND HORTON HEAT: I think the music in the mid 20th century will live forever, because music recording was still a new phenomenon. "New technology" would be the best way to say it. So, there was an explosion of music – starting with the early recordings of big band and country singers. And then they eventually had the explosion of black artists.

Because nowadays, there's so much music out there, that it's easy for people like me to just give up. And I have. I've given up. I've said, "*Screw it.*" When there's this many new recordings that are coming out all the time, I know there's a lot of cool stuff out there that I'm missing, but to find and weed out all the cool stuff that's coming out now…it's mind-boggling.

So, for that reason, a lot of people that had big hit songs from the mid 20th century…those will live forever. But a lot of this new stuff, there's just *too much* stuff. I mean, I'm not saying that the new stuff is not as good as the old stuff, but there's just too much of it. We've got so much music.

That's why right now, we're on a Christmas tour, and pretty much because when recording technology exploded, there were so many Christmas songs that came out, that there's really not much room for any new Christmas songs to get as big as "Baby It's Cold Outside" and "White Christmas." So, in that respect, Hendrix will live forever – as far as a guitar player, his songs, and music.

Chapter 13
Modern Day Shred King
Talks Jimi

Dream Theater guitarist John Petrucci has long been considered one of the top shredders in metal. But he has never been interviewed at length about Jimi and what his guitar playing meant to him...and also, to other similarly-styled players.

How important was Jimi to the evolution of rock guitar?

Incredibly important. Because nobody saw anything or heard anything like that up until him. It was just kind of like, there are certain points where there is a paradigm shift in the world of music – and in this case, in guitar. And him coming on the scene playing the way he did...*nobody* did that. So, it was like, "What the hell is this?" Now, of course, it must have been ridiculous to experience that in person at the time. We can only think back and go back and look at a video or read about things. But I can imagine. Just think about what is going on at that time musically, and then think about the music of Jimi Hendrix and the videos that you've seen. It stands out as being *completely* groundbreaking.

Some metal guitarists have been critical of Jimi's tuning problems after using the whammy bar so much, and not playing very fast. Can you look past his "faults" as a guitar player?

Oh, yeah – it's not about that. He wasn't playing modern day shred guitar. He was doing something that was really based on raw, organic rock distorted guitar feel – that was never done before. So, the use of bending, whammy bar, and stuff like that – it was done in a way that was unique, and again, groundbreaking. I don't think it's fair to have any sort of criticism as, "Oh, the string slightly went out of tune." All that was part of it. All the noise, feedback.

I mean, you're pushing amplifiers at *ridiculous* volumes and breaking up speakers – not in a way that we do it now, which is controlled with high gain amplifiers. But in a way where you actually had to push the amp beyond its abilities and its speakers. And all that noise, feedback, and the stuff going out of tune, bending, and whammy bar stuff…that's all part of the charm and the vibe that Jimi Hendrix had. If anything, you don't want to just homogenize that into being all in-tune, perfect, and noiseless – that wouldn't be Jimi.

What aspect of Jimi's playing do you admire most?

I've always admired the way that he was a songwriter and guitar player – and he accompanied himself in that way at the same time. So, not just a guitar player in a band or anything like that – he kind of seemed to seamlessly weave in the song to his singing to the guitar. It was all one big thing. And I've always admired something like that. Certainly, it's not anything that I can do.

I've read that when you first heard "Voodoo Child," you thought it was an original by Stevie Ray Vaughan!

Of course, I had heard some of the popular stuff that was on the radio growing up in New York and Long Island. But I don't think that "Voodoo Child" was really played on the radio. I didn't really hear it. So, when I heard Stevie Ray Vaughan's version, I'm like, *"This is awesome."* I had no idea that there was a Hendrix version...which, shame on me! But, the first time I heard Stevie's version was the first time I heard that song.

Is it possible that in a roundabout way, Jimi may have seeped into your playing a little bit through you being a fan of Stevie Ray Vaughan?

Oh, no doubt. Absolutely.

Do you think if Jimi would have lived, he would have perhaps gotten more "technical" with his guitar playing, and embraced modern day technology?

I think he might have gotten more into the pedals and things that have been developed. Sure. Because obviously, it was something he was into. I don't know stylistically if he would have moved away from what he was doing to get into something more technical. He didn't seem like that type of player to me – from what I saw. So, who knows? My guess would be not. I would picture him getting more into "sound design" – based on the different technologies developed since then.

What do you think modern day shredders and guitarists could learn or pick up from Jimi?

Everything from rhythm accompaniment to the importance of a solo's role within a song structure – and how it makes it something that actually carries a song along. And not just some "noodle-y moment" that you could live without. He always had the ability to where you looked forward to that solo moment – it actually brought the emotion of the song up to another level.

What does Jimi Hendrix mean to you as a guitar player?

To me, it kind of goes back to your first question. He's somebody who established a style and a direction of a style that wasn't there before. And probably really spring-boarded what a lot of modern day rock and metal guitar playing and attitude would turn into. I mean, there are guys today that still play using the influence that he had – whether it's in your actual playing and licks, or going for a certain type of sound…like, "What would Jimi do?" It's *still* relevant. It's not like it's this old, vintage-y thing that nobody has any need for any more. So, that's amazing. When somebody does that, then they're a pioneer – when it still is relevant, so many years later.

Chapter 14
Psychedelia

Was there ever a psychedelic icon as big as Jimi?

BILLY SHEEHAN: Absolutely not. And if there are any, I believe they took the cue from Jimi. Amongst his peers, there were people that were *kind of* along those lines – Janis Joplin, the Stones, the Beatles. They were trendsetters in so many ways. But Jimi stepped out from everybody and did something that was incredibly unique and I don't think there's ever been anyone to spell out that era.

Especially the *Electric Ladyland* record, which is really the culmination of the two records that came before it and where he was headed in the future, too. "1983" – me and my friends would listen to that song *over and over and over*. To this day, I think I know every note in my mind. Jimi was "the man" and he set the stage for a lot of changes in the world.

RANDY HANSEN: I don't think anybody is even close. He's the king of psychedelia – if anything. Nobody was more psychedelic than that guy! A lot of people tried but it seemed like everybody who tried used elements that he already used. If anybody was close to it, it was the Beatles. I mean, if "Revolution #9" isn't psychedelic, then I don't know what psychedelic is! Just the utilization and the manipulation of sound to the ends of trying to sound almost drug-induced – that to me is psychedelia.

CURT KIRKWOOD: The Beatles definitely had

their own way of doing that – and it's amazing that they were teen idols and then decided to go for it, but still, they had the "band mentality," and it wasn't as freeform. There's moments of it for sure where the eyes kind of roll back in the head – when Jimi's just going for it.

I'd imagine quite a bit [that drugs played a role in the creation of Jimi's music]. *Are You Experienced* kind of says it all – either you have or you haven't. When I was younger, another influence was, "Hey, *let's do like Jimi did.*" And I know that Gong and Daevid Allen did some stuff where they were all dosed during the recordings. But I kind of assumed that all those guys just lit up in the studio. So, that was a big influence for our first record [1982's *Meat Puppets*]. It was just like, "Let's make sure that we're tripping for everything we lay down – for better or worse."

Oh, it doesn't matter. [In response to the question, "As far as your experiences, do you enjoy listening to Jimi's music stoned or not stoned?"] *I like it.* My enjoyment of music has always been kind of free of that. I can enjoy stuff, but I saw the Grateful Dead a number of times, and I'll go back and say, "Jerry Garcia is a different guitar player. But in terms of somebody that was good at paving a trip with music, that band was good at it." They did a lot of musical experimentation with that influence. It shaped that band – and San Francisco bands, in general.

I saw the Grateful Dead a number of times and I think once or twice I was tripping when I saw them. And I didn't have to be – they were really good at it. I saw Carlos Santana one time in my late teens, where I dropped a hit of acid – and that was *fucking sick*. And I think it helped. Somebody told me that he was on acid in the *Woodstock* movie – you can kind of tell. But you don't have to be.

FRANK MARINO: Well psychedelia, yeah – but certainly not with the guitar. I mean, psychedelia is kind of *a sound*, right? So you could say that some of Pink Floyd's stuff was psychedelic. We had records by bands called Ultimate Spinach that we thought were psychedelic, OK? [Laughs] "Psychedelic music" was a type of music that went with the posters from the Avalon Ballroom and the Fillmore. You could even say the Dead was kind of psychedelic – when they did stuff like "Dark Star." But no – certainly not with a guitar. These are watershed sort of moments, where a person was able to make a guitar do things other than what a guitar does.

I'll let you in on a very interesting conversation I once had with Richie Havens – who played Woodstock and knew Jimi Hendrix fairly well. I happened to become friends with Richie at one point – because I did gigs with him. And I was having a conversation with him one day, we were talking about Jimi Hendrix's influence on guitar and what kind of guitarist he was. And he said something really interesting to me – "Jimi didn't play the guitar. *He played the amplifier*." And it suddenly became clear to me that he was describing exactly what Jimi Hendrix really is.

Because really good guitar players – like Steve Vai or whomever – if they actually classify someone as a "good guitarist" or "great guitarist," there is a number of criteria that they use by which to say that about a guy. For instance, they may say that about a guy who is very adept or he's fast or he's got great vibrato or something – there's something technical about it.

But Jimi Hendrix…it's an odd thing, because he's credited as being one of the greatest – if not *the* greatest – guitarists of all-time. Especially in rock. But yet, when anyone does "the Jimi Hendrix impression," they almost always play lightning-fast licks. And yet, you can't find a single song or solo where Jimi Hendrix played fast. And most people don't realize that – even *fans of Hendrix* don't realize that. But if you go looking into all of Hendrix's material, with possibly the exception of one part of a solo in "Machine Gun," he has absolutely *never* played fast lines – anything more than eighth notes or sixteenth notes.

Nobody ever noticed that, and yet, they'll credit him as the greatest of all-time as a guitarist – and I stress the "ist" part of it. But that's not exactly what he was. He was a groundbreaking inventor of a new way of looking at an instrument, and putting it across to people. He gets credit for it, but he sort of gets credit in the wrong way. You go to a music store, and there's a poster of Jimi Hendrix with the arm up in the air with the guitar. But that's not really what Jimi Hendrix was. That's sort of what *the industry* thought he was.

And I'm reminded of having known his career early and lived through it – his rise and his death – from an article that came out in *Rolling Stone*, when *Rolling Stone* was a newspaper. And I'll never forget the headline one day, which said, "JIMI

HENDRIX: 'I DON'T WANT TO BE A CLOWN ANYMORE'." And this was just before things changed and he died.

I think that Jimi Hendrix himself may have come to the point where he realized that the over-accentuation of his "rock-ness" – the rock star thing of burning guitars and being a wild man – wasn't really ever what he wanted to do. And I see stories, I hear people who talk about it – how the burning of the instrument really wasn't his idea, it was some roadie's idea to compete with the Who.

It makes a lot of sense, because I think first and foremost, Jimi Hendrix was a composer, and guitar happened to be his instrument for composition, and I think that maybe he was a little bit miscast as the "rock star in the cape." And I think he didn't like that. I just think there is this weird misconception about who he is…or who he was – and about his approach to music and about how he actually used the guitar and played it. And I think when we sit down as guitar players and actually analyze it, we find, "Hey…why didn't we ever notice that before?"

Jimi Hendrix is not a technically proficient guitarist – in terms of the "ist" part. He probably couldn't do nearly what Steve Vai, Joe Satriani, or Allan Holdsworth could do. But yet, he's still the greatest. He truly is. And they'll say so, too. So, you have to wonder what they mean when they say that. I think what they mean is his inventiveness and sound. A lot of people can play Jimi Hendrix's tunes, and even if they play them exactly right – and I do know how to play them exactly right – they don't sound like him. *No matter what*. Even if you use his equipment.

So, there's a certain uniqueness to what he was doing, and it's the sum of all the parts that make up what he is – whether it was left-handed and the Strat, his approach, and everything else. He added together all his influences – and you get Jimi Hendrix. Throw in a bit of psychedelic drugs – that may have had something to do with it, too!

MICHAEL SCHENKER: Jimi Hendrix was very spaced out – he was out there. And there was a lot of bad stuff he did – when he wasn't together. I guess it depends on what kind of drugs he was taking when he was playing! But today when I look at Jimi Hendrix, he definitely was a natural genius – there is no doubt about it. I did do an interview and a little bit of guitar playing in Jimi Hendrix's apartment in London, so I actually was in his apartment – where he lived for two or three years.

RIK EMMETT: His manager, Chas Chandler, I think said, "Look Jimi, this is what we're going to do. You're going to get your afro going, we're going to have posters of you with the big afro, it's going to be psychedelic, and you're going to be *this guy*. I want you to do all that stuff – I want you to put the guitar between your legs, drop it on the floor, set it on fire." That sort of captured the imagination of the counterculture around the world – which was already this kind of "hippie drug culture thing," with peace and love and all of that.

He became this iconic symbol of peace and love and I'm not sure that can ever happen again. And I don't mean to discredit his abilities or his musicianship at all, by saying that – to make it seem that it was just this cultural kind of thing. Because it wasn't. It was a combination of those two things.

I think [journalist] Malcolm Gladwell talked about this point, that somebody is going to come along and sort of be the right thing at the right place at the right time. And in a way, with electric guitar and the whole peace and love thing, Hendrix was the right thing at the right place at the right time. So, he kind of became the iconic hero of all of that.

BRUCE KULICK: Well, I don't only think of Hendrix as that genre. But certainly, he is a big part of that. He would probably be…that and the *Sgt. Pepper/Magical Mystery Tour* Beatles era would be my biggest thoughts when it comes to psychedelia. Yeah, there's the Jefferson Airplane and other bands of psychedelic kind of things – but there was something about how he presented himself.

BRIAN TATLER: I mean, the Beatles were pretty special, and John Lennon. But no, I think Hendrix was the full package.

RIK EMMETT: Canada is a different kind of a market, because it's a very large country, with a relatively small population in contrast to the States and England, which has an incredible amount of intensity there – in terms of the size of it versus the population. I think it's a little easier to have a thing like Beatlemania – and later, Hendrixmania – occur in a place like England, than it is to tap into in Canada. Besides that, the other thing to think about is the counterculture.

There was something about Hendrix where he was very much "the love child," "the rainbow warrior" – there was this thing about Hendrix and drugs and hippies. And in Canada, the scene had not really evolved away from AM radio being the dominant force. So, until Hendrix, there was a little bit of the "Foxy Lady" or "Purple Haze" kind of thing, but it probably didn't have the same impact that it had in the States – where FM radio had a little more influence, and was gaining more all the time. But he did come to Canada to play on tour.

RANDY HANSEN: He had *maniacal* fashion. Mostly, he dressed different at school, because half his family tree was Indian, and his grandma was making him stuff – handmade clothes and vests and stuff. And he was wearing them to school. So, Jimi was looking different right from the get-go. As soon as he entered junior high probably, everyone was looking at him like, *"What the hell?"* He was probably more like a hippie before there were hippies!

BRUCE KULICK: There's something about his connection to London and being in England. But his history there was very important – he was considered almost part of the British Invasion, even though he's American. In some ways, he was the only really powerful American that was so influential.

Because the other artists that definitely turned my head inside out and upside down were British – the Beatles, Led Zeppelin, the Who, Cream. Even from the Moody Blues to Yes – they were *all* British bands. It was crazy. That's why I loved

Mountain – I liked that they were an "American Cream." Grand Funk I was fascinated with, too.

But getting back to Hendrix, there he was in London – Carnaby Street. Watch an *Austin Powers* movie – you'll see what I mean! That was where fashion was very important. He owned it. Coming from R&B and playing with Curtis Knight, the Isley Brothers, and whatever his history was as an R&B guitarist, clearly you see how being dressed and presenting yourself on stage is important. And then of course, as soon as there was a free-for-all, you could be as flamboyant as you wanted – a la *Asylum*-era Kiss. But he did it with incredible style.

I still love every picture I see – you can't help but look at the clothes he was wearing. And it was *a statement* back then – look at Cream in the beginning. Alright, Clapton survived and got over his heroin habit, but years later, he just looks like a guy shopping at a leisure store. But look at the psychedelic pictures of Cream back then. So, it was very "en vogue."

And since Hendrix had his guys look that way – from Mitch Mitchell and Noel Redding…I bet it was odd for Billy Cox to be in hippie fashionable clothes, being his army buddy and not growing up in London with him. But I think the clothes were fantastic. I remember I think it was Eric Singer bought me one year for my birthday one of those replica purple Jimi Hendrix hats – because he knows I love Jimi.

RICHARD LLOYD: I think when he went over to England, it was *bursting* with fashion. He got that military jacket that he wore a lot. People were making him clothes – private people. Then in New York, there was a shop called Granny Takes a Trip that he shopped at often – y'know, crushed red velvet pants, really beautiful color coordination. He had a personal style that was beautiful.

FRANK MARINO: Well, that night [that Frank saw Jimi in Montreal during 1968], he was wearing red pants – and I'll never forget it, because they were *bright* red. Who wore red pants in those days? You might have seen it at a circus or something, y'know? And you could notice it from so far away – and I'm talking fire engine red, here. But I always thought that his clothing was cool after that – it's not just a question of the colors, but I always thought he had very unique clothes.

They always looked a little bit different than everybody else, and quite honestly, they looked like the kind of clothes that a guy would actually wear not just because he was on stage, but those were the clothes he wore. I thought that was pretty cool. For most of the music industry, guys get in costume to go on stage, and you see them after the show and they're wearing t-shirts and jeans. But I'm sort of in the same vein now – I always wear on stage what I wear anyway. So, I'm kind of like that – I like to wear what I normally wear.

RIK EMMETT: He was the poster child. You can still go to t-shirt and poster sites, and there's Jimi. The whole of like...a rainbow warrior, a psychedelic hero – *he was the total package.*

Chapter 15
What Made Jimi "Jimi"?

The factors that made Jimi stand out from the pack.

DON FELDER: He was a magnetic, powerful, creative force, that was pretty much unequaled for that time period. And you knew it the minute you heard his guitar sound – whatever record it was on, whatever radio station – as soon as you heard him play, you knew who it was. Extremely unique identity as a guitarist. But everybody has an extremely unique identity as a guitarist. And if you don't, then you haven't been able to develop your own style, your own tone, and your own phrasing – then you've just become a copycat that does covers of other people.

I was at the Metropolitan Museum of Art, where Jimi Hendrix's Strat that he played at Woodstock is on display. I think Steve Miller got up and spoke, and he said how unique everyone who picks up the guitar plays and sounds. One time, I was sitting in a studio, and Joe Walsh had just come back, and he brought this new guitar and he had a new pedal. He was just sitting in the studio messing around, and I said, "That sounds great! Let me play that." I took the same guitar through the same pedal...and it sounded like *me*. It's the Indian, not the arrow.

So, everybody that picks up a guitar – how they phrase, their finger movements, how they pluck the string – has a unique identity. But Hendrix was so unbelievably different and unique for his time, that he stood out everywhere he went – on stage, on the radio, wherever it was, it was just magical.

ALEX LIFESON: No one came close to playing with the feel, passion, and intensity at that time. It was otherworldly and innovative.

REVEREND HORTON HEAT: He kind of came on the scene and cut everybody. In some ways, I think that was kind of a fault of his – he could cut anybody, he could go out there and bring down the house so hard no matter what the dude did. It was hard to follow. And that was *the Who*, y'know? Pete Townshend has a little bit of a bitterness about Jimi Hendrix, because they loved Hendrix, and they got him on the Monterey Pop Festival.

And the Who's big shtick at the time was breaking their instruments. And that show that Hendrix tore up his guitar and when he lit it on fire, the guys in the Who were kind of pissed. Lead guitar players can be really mean, because man, if they can, they'll cut you. That was an interesting time in music. But I don't really like it that much when I see somebody tear up a guitar. I think, "Wow. That's a guitar that some young kid could learn to play on."

BRIAN TATLER: Incredible sounds and confidence. And what a brilliant performer! Absolutely charismatic. I've watched him many times in videos, and I always look for Hendrix videos. He always looks amazing on stage – sexy, flamboyant with his clothes. At the time, it was probably like something from another planet. It must have been like a bomb going off in London when he suddenly appeared amongst the '60s crowd – where everybody was looking at the Beatles and the Stones.

And then suddenly, Hendrix appeared – playing an upside down Fender Strat. So, I can only imagine the shock that went 'round everyone. What an incredible player. No one played like that at the time. The way he used feedback and wah – things that we had not really heard before. That kind of sustain and the way he used the tremolo arm. It must have been incredible to be there.

RANDY HANSEN: His sci-fi sounds. His delivery – the way that he sold every note to you. If you were at a Jimi Hendrix concert, he's up there, and he's maybe not meaning to, but man…if anybody ever sold the guitar to mainstream America, it was Jimi. More than anyone I can think of. Holding that guitar upside down – a right-handed guitar played left-handed.

And I point this out to people, too – when he played with his teeth, as soon as he starts flipping that guitar up, you see the *sexy part* of that Stratocaster, not the dumb part that the right-handers have to show if they try to play with their teeth. But everything was just a touch better with him, y'know? I think that's why he set the bar so high – because he was not only a great guitar player and performer, but also, a great teacher. And wise beyond his years. The superlatives for Jimi are just endless.

REVEREND HORTON HEAT: I was a blues kid, and Jimi Hendrix was basically just a blues guy that cranked it up and got a little more psychedelic. But the base of it all, it was still blues. But he took guitar playing into another realm. And a lot of it was the amount of distortion. He wasn't afraid to crank out his fuzz box and the Marshall, and get these tones that were really similar to a saxophone. So, he could hit a note, and it would just keep ringing and sustaining, and he could bend it up and bend it down, which is very much like something a saxophone would do – not a guitar. That style of guitar playing was really very, very different.

There was a guy that I talked to recently – he's quite a bit older than me – and he talked about how back before Hendrix, nobody really bent notes that much. They would bend them *a little bit*. I think Hendrix may have used a little bit thinner strings. I don't think he used a wound G-string – which meant he could bend that thing even more.

But those wild saxophone-type lines and bends were really different from the way he played when he was with Little Richard and that other stuff – he was just more bluesy, and not nearly as turned up with this distortion and sustain. It made his instrument really, really versatile. When you add something that you couldn't do before, it's always going to be something kind of cool. The reaction I think in general was, "Wow. I can't believe he makes a guitar sound like *that*."

BILLY SHEEHAN: I always refer to him as "the coolest guy that ever lived." Because he was *cool*. He didn't get excited on stage – he'd just say something on the mic. He wouldn't get excited or upset – just laidback and cool, he knew what he was doing, confident, bang, bang, bang. I just thought he was the coolest human being that ever lived.

179 WHAT MADE JIMI "JIMI"?

DOUG PINNICK: I've read different books about him, and the last one I read [2010's *Becoming Jimi Hendrix*, by Steven Roby and Brad Schreiber], they put together a whole book about his life with his family, and who he was. It wasn't when he got famous in England and all these stories that everybody knows. It was stories about him personally – about how when his mom died, his dad wouldn't let him and his brother go to the funeral, but he gave them whiskey instead – when they were kids. He was like, "This is how men deal with death." And his aunt was saying that every now and then, she would look on the back porch, and Jimi would just be sitting out there, crying. And she would say, "Jimi, what's wrong?" And he would say, "I miss my mom."

I understand that. I immediately related to him, and the more I started learning about him, the more I related to his lyrics – "I Don't Live Today" or "Angel," or the songs that come from your heart being broken by the person that you love the most. And then, his brother telling us stories about "Spanish Castle Magic" – that was a nightclub. His lyrics were true stories – Spanish Castle was the name of the place. All those songs – "Crosstown Traffic." I remember reading a story about his girlfriend saying that when he played Bob Dylan, the record changed his whole life.

RANDY HANSEN: Jimi's dad [Al Hendrix] was a wonderful guy. He was such a sweet man. He used to show up at a lot of my shows. If I was playing anywhere near him, he was there a lot. And we'd always end up at the end of the night standing in a corner, with people fielding him questions. It was really lovely to be around him. He was such a nice guy. You could tell where Jimi came from – he raised Jimi with an iron paddle though, y'know? He was a real disciplinarian. My dad was a little like that, too. It's better to have someone like that, than – like Ted Nugent would say – a dishrag.

RIK EMMETT: Looking back in retrospect and based on columns that I've done, I believe that Hendrix – at heart – was a better rhythm guitar player than most lead guitar players. So, he had a sense of songs and the rhythm of parts. I think you can probably trace that back to when he was a sideman playing that Chitlin' Circuit stuff and being in R&B bands. He had a real "R&B kind of flavor" to the blues and the songs that he created in order to carry the blues – that was a huge part of who he was.

In these circumstances, if somebody asks me that question, I always say, "He was one of the greatest rhythm guitar players of rock." He just had a unique approach to it. He had that Curtis Mayfield kind of...where you strike a chord, and you're going from the second up to the third inside the chord, and those kinds of little things.

And he had such big hands that he was very graceful about using his thumb, for example – for bass notes. When he played "Little Wing," and he played a bass note, there's a chord that's sliding from a Fadd9 to a Gadd9 and then back to an Fadd9. Meanwhile, his thumb is holding down the bass G the whole time.

And so, I ask your average good guitar player, "Go ahead and try that. See if you can get your thumb to stay in one place, when you slide two frets back down from it!" And he did it like it was *nothing*. His thumb could come up around the top and do things...because his was so big and his fingers were so long. Those are some of the things I would say – rhythm player, physical kinds of gifts.

I think he was probably the first guitar player that ever really took such huge advantage of the tremolo arm on a Strat and skinny strings – so you could bend the crap out of them. Yes, James Burton had done it years before and started the revolution of putting skinny banjo strings on guitars, and moving all the strings up one, so you'd have a really skinny set. But Hendrix did that, too – to the nth degree. Jimmy Page was also a guy who would do over-bending and made a big deal out of it.

But Hendrix was the guy that was making it talk in ways that very few other guys did. Hendrix was probably the sole source of every guy having to go out and get a wah wah. [Laughs] It's like, any guitar player worth his salt was like, "Well, I've got to get a wah wah. I've got to make it talk *like Jimi*." He was the start of so many things.

MICHAEL SCHENKER: Woodstock – that was the bang of the new musical revolution. It was the big bang of new music. So many bands came out of that – Mountain, Santana, Jimi Hendrix, and all of these guys. And people discovered it, because that festival was so successful, and so many people went there, and it was '69, and it was drugs and it was being free spirited and hippie and carefree. All of that together. It was a time that everybody really got fascinated – including the music that was going on. I think it had a lot of impact on everything at that point. And then people like Jimi Hendrix, Leslie West, and Carlos Santana – they kind of stuck out.

Jimi Hendrix was one of the them, and that was when I think Jimi Hendrix had developed into that guitarist that was revolutionary – that was kind of completely "out there." It was like something nobody had ever done before...or it was playing that was coming from where nobody had ever heard. I think he was doing what I was doing all these years – he was playing from within. I don't know what his roots were, I don't know what he was influenced by – if I studied it, maybe I could understand the connection – but I also got inspired by Jeff Beck, Jimmy Page, and Eric Clapton.

But at some point, I made up my mind that I wanted to create within. And maybe that's what Jimi Hendrix did, as well. And he probably also used drugs to be able to do that – to play from within. So, what he was doing was coming from a world that nobody was familiar with – that sound and that way of playing and being so carefree. Very good at improvising and just being "in the moment." I think that's what it was – being in the moment.

But I don't know if it had to do with drugs or it had to do with him...I don't know how he did it, because I didn't study Jimi Hendrix. But this is what I imagine, because he had good times and bad times – I've found that, because I've heard some really bad guitar playing, but we all had that. But I think he had that more extreme, because of maybe doing too much of something. I mean, if somebody is completely drunk, then obviously, you play bad. It goes without saying. But he is one of a kind. And I think that is the strength of Jimi Hendrix – a one of a kind.

RON "BUMBLEFOOT" THAL: Jimi came from the time when music was very *human* – there was no Autotune, there was no quantizing. There was none of that stuff. It was about reality. When people played live and are really putting on a show, the instrument will go out of tune. And to me, that's not a problem – *that's character*.

I've heard things from AC/DC and Led Zeppelin that wasn't exactly in 440, but all the greatest, most legendary bands were not always perfectly in tune. And if anything, that little bit of tension gave it humanity and that's the thing that we love. We shouldn't be striving for perfection – we should be striving for that once in a lifetime moment, where things aren't perfect, and you're capturing something that will never happen the same way again. So, I love that part of it.

KIM THAYIL: Shredder guitarists are into speed and proficiency. It's very athletically-oriented – as opposed to aesthetically-oriented. Not to say that there is no aesthetic content to be emphasized in the technical proficiency of what we do. And there were people that were interested in that when I was a teen. Hendrix certainly showed proficiency, but he also showed improvisational skills, spontaneity, and soul – and interpreting the pieces they're going to play by mood or by aesthetic decisions he made when he did covers. Those are elements of playing guitar. But feedback may suggest "noise" to someone who is into a particular clarity of overtones and harmonics.

CURT KIRKWOOD: He would let the guitar do the talking and let the amp have an effect on the guitar. I'd grown up listening Mahavishnu, and like I said, I'd heard Hendrix. But I liked Mahavishnu and John McLaughlin in terms of somebody that was really a dead-on technical great player, and still, had a bit of shred in there. I knew I wasn't trying to do that. I never liked to practice that much. [Laughs]

I more liked playing with the guys and seeing what kind of noises that we could make. And to see this one guy just open it up there – you don't hear that with just about anything else. Not until later – when you start to hear it for sure in some of the avant-punk stuff. Hendrix is the only guy that I think about in that way. Because Mahavishnu wouldn't have been Mahavishnu if Hendrix hadn't have come on the scene.

EAST BAY RAY: It was like, "Keep it catchy...*but think outside the box.*" The famous songwriter, Cole Porter, he had a line – one of the things he tried to do was "Make the familiar sound different, and make the different sound familiar." I think that's why the songs last for so long, and I think that's definitely with Hendrix. It was just outside atonal jazz, but he would pass through episodes of that. And similar to the Dead Kennedys – there are episodes that are *really* outside, and then we pass through it but go somewhere else.

I think most musicians in rock music are like that [unable to read or write music]. I know very few people that read and write traditionally. My father had a book on the delta blues, and the guy was trying to put the blues into notation. [Laughs] And he did this added thing, because the timing is a little different and the pitch is a little different than what you can write in traditional form.

RANDY HANSEN: Of course, I'm a guitar player and I love playing guitar, and I really love playing Jimi's music. But I think the real reason I keep doing this isn't that, and has nothing to do with that – as much as it has to do with turning people on to the ideas that Jimi Hendrix had. A lot of people only know those few songs of his – the ones that were on the radio. And they're really attracted to those.

But I really don't know why anyone would stop there. I certainly didn't. I think if they were to *really* discover what the guy was trying to tell everyone, they'd find a lot of peace and love and understanding. It might help them – because it really helped me. After my father was gone and I was rudderless...*he became my rudder*.

KIRK HAMMETT: I sincerely think that Jimi Hendrix invented heavy metal – with that first Jimi Hendrix album. Cream...they were on to something. The Jeff Beck Group...they were on to something. The Yardbirds...they were on to something. But it was Jimi that really, really brought it all together and created the example that everyone else followed. And if you look at what happened post-Hendrix – '71/'72 – the musical trends were to be progressive and heavy. Which is exactly what Jimi Hendrix was *already*.

A lot of the albums that came out around then by a lot of bands – Zeppelin, Yes, Jethro Tull, Sabbath, Purple – they wanted to be heavy. Post-

Jimi, they put out heavier albums. Because that's what people wanted and that was the trend. You could see that there and then how much of an influence musically he had on his peers.

EAST BAY RAY: It's not heavy metal, it's not punk rock, it's not Bob Seger rock...*what would you call it?*

Chapter 16
The Other Guitarist
That Played With
Mitch, Noel, Buddy & Billy

*Who else played with both of Jimi's best-known
rhythm sections?*

·RANDY HANSEN: I got to play with Mitch,
Buddy, Billy, and Noel. I even got to put together a
band that never was – which was Buddy Miles, Noel
Redding, and myself. That was kind of strange,
because every time we'd launch into a Band of
Gypsys song, I had to teach Noel the Band of Gypsys
stuff. Like, I started playing "Who Knows" – we
jammed on it and then he came over to me, and said,
"Is that one of *yours?*" Which told me that once he
left the group, he stopped listening. He had a little
chip on his shoulder about it.

A lot of stuff would have happened, but those
two guys were really funny…you find some people
that have been through the business that have been
majorly affected by it – and majorly screwed by it –
they have a little chip on their shoulder, and they're
not so ready to just jump right back into it.

When I was playing with Buddy for a while,
his manager was messing with everyone's money
and not paying people. He wasn't paying me. They
got Billy Cox on the phone, and they wanted me to
talk him into playing with us. And they put me on the
phone with him, and I said, "The only way I'll talk to
him is if you guys are all out of the room."

So, I kicked everybody out of the room, went

and talked to him, and I very quietly told him, "You don't want to come. What are you doing now for money?" He said, "I've got a very lucrative job – I'm an insurance salesman." I said, "They're already messing with my money." And really, it's a good thing I did this, because at the end of the tour, they got Mitch Mitchell to fill in for Buddy – who had gotten thrown back in jail for parole violation. That's how I ended up with Mitch Mitchell. And that was just a done deal – there was nothing I could do with that. But this was something that I could head-off before it got started.

I wanted to play with Billy *really* badly. I told him, "I really want to play with you Billy, but I would advise you not to come, because they're not going to pay you. And you're going to end up in litigation with them" – which I did. Now, I just went ahead and chanced it, anyway. But I was not about to be responsible for bringing someone else into it. Especially somebody who I admired so much. I just came out of the room and said, "I don't know if he's coming or not." He took my advice.

The only time I played with him was when they opened EMP [now known as MoPOP] here in Seattle, and I played with everybody – Buddy, Billy, Noel, and Mitch. We all played at the same time. Actually, at the rehearsal, we played the whole *Band of Gypsys* record – with just Buddy, Billy, and myself – while everyone else in the room just stood around, watching.

I know that album like the back of my hand – I quit school to play along to that record! So, I know pretty much *every note* – except for the notes in "Machine Gun." I can't get them all, because some of them…I just don't know how he's doing it. I probably should slow the record down, but I don't want to cheat that way. I can't figure out what he's doing, and his timing is so unusual – it's just great. If there was ever a live masterpiece, it is "Machine Gun."

And when I walked off stage after that, there was a guy interviewing me for *Guitar Player Magazine*, and he said, "How does it feel to have your hand in the glove of Jimi Hendrix?" I was like, "*I like how you said that.*" [Laughs]

Chapter 17
Jimi & Frank

Two of Zappa's guitarists compare their former band leader to Hendrix.

ADRIAN BELEW: To me, there's not that much comparison in what they did. There are some blues-based things in Frank's early guitar playing, but overall, Frank's interest seemed to do with fitting rhythms over odd time signatures using strange nasally guitar sounds. He liked awkward sounds! Frank's use of the wah wah was about as close to Hendrix as he got in my mind.

By the time I played with Frank, he was in a different phase of his playing. He had a huge refrigerator full of pretty advanced gear, so he was experimenting with sounds as Jimi would have, but with a different approach. He was not the same type of player.

One of my favorite moments with Frank was when we were playing in Atlanta on the anniversary of Jimi's death [at the Fox Theater, on September 18, 1977]. True to form, out of nowhere Frank turned to me and said, *"Do your Hendrix thing!"* I attempted some crazy feedback and gave it my best!

STEVE VAI: Hendrix was one of Frank's contemporaries. So there was a different dialogue there – it wasn't like…sacred to Frank. Hendrix – I think to Frank – was a great guitar player that was doing some pretty cool things. *The end.* You could never really get Frank to elaborate on it. Frank liked to take the piss out of things he actually liked, sometimes. I remember once, I believe he really liked Al Di Meola, so he would occasionally take the piss out of the way Al played. [Laughs] But it didn't stop him from inviting Al to come join us to jam at a show in New York in 1980.

So, by the same token, I remember my first rehearsal with Frank, he was writing a song called "We're Turning Again," and there was one line in it that was, "Jimi come back and feedback on my knapsack" or something like that. And at that point, I was supposed to turn around and bring the guitar up to the amp and do a feedback solo.

And I do know that Frank acquired a guitar that Jimi burnt in Miami at one of those festivals. Now, any other person that received a guitar that Jimi Hendrix burned, they would probably put it in a glass case and leave it exactly the way it was. It's sacred ground. But Frank saw it as a cool-looking body, and just completely gutted it and put whatever he wanted in it – to make it work the way he wanted it. I used that Hendrix guitar on the second European tour every night.

So, there's an irreverence there, but it's a *quiet* irreverence in a sense. It's actually a normal flow of appreciation – as opposed to God-like status.

Chapter 18
NYC

As a co-founder of Television (who along with the likes of the Ramones, the Talking Heads, Patti Smith, and Blondie, were part of the first wave of punk bands to hail from CBGB's) and forming a winning guitar tandem with Tom Verlaine, Richard Lloyd's contribution to rock guitar is significant. And it turns out that he also crossed paths with Jimi quite a bit in NYC circa the late '60s. Here, Richard remembers...

I've heard that you became a friend of Jimi's, but did you get to see him perform live before meeting him?

Yeah. I got to meet him later on. The first time we went to see him, my friend Velvert [Turner] and I, we went backstage after the show was over to say hello, but they wouldn't let us in to see Jimi, because he was vomiting in a bucket – because he had been on a rotating stage, and it made him dizzy. They promised him that the stage moves so slow that he'd never notice it, but obviously, that didn't work – because he was deathly ill. So, we didn't get to see him.

Velvert already knew him, so, I was just a tag-along. I must have been 16. There wasn't much I had to say to the guy. I just wanted to be nearby – like a fly on the wall. I don't know where it was, to tell you the truth. I know that it wasn't in Manhattan – it was in Queens, somewhere. We had to take a subway there. [Note: It was probably the Singer Bowl in Queens, on August 23, 1968]

How did you first meet Jimi?

We used to see him walking down the street with his girlfriend – because he took an apartment on 12th Street in Manhattan, in the Village, and I grew up in the Village. After school, we would hang out at a sandwich shop, and Jimi would pass by – he lived one block away. In New York, you don't saddle up to celebrities and try to talk to them. But we would yell out, "Hey Jimi! How's it going?" And he would say back, "How's it going, guys?" Stuff like that. So, I saw him before I actually met him. It must have been at one of his shows that we did get backstage, and got to say hello – it was Velvert mostly, I kept my mouth shut. So, I saw him a number of times.

      The very first time I saw him, I guess it was at that revolving stage show, and a couple of things I remember about it was one, it was like looking into a nuclear reactor. It was unlike anything I ever experienced before – in terms of music. The other thing was with the revolving stage, the people who could see him that were in front of the stage would stand up. And then as the thing rotated, they would sit back down when they couldn't see them anymore, and then the new people would stand up. It was the first "wave" I ever saw in a stadium – I thought that was kind of hilarious.

If you wouldn't mind explaining who Velvert is for people who don't know, and how you met him.

I was at a friend's house – we were waiting to score some hashish. The phone rang, and we thought it was that. But my friend, Zeke – it was his house – got on the phone, and said, "Oh no. This kid's coming over – he says he knows Jimi Hendrix. We should all laugh at him. *Nobody* knows Jimi Hendrix." So, the door opened, and Velvert was there. I lay eyes on him, and I knew immediately he *did* know Jimi Hendrix. I don't know how I knew...I just knew. And the interesting thing was everybody was like, "Prove it to us." So, he said, "Jimi's in town – I'll call him at his hotel."

We went into another room where the phone was, and it rang and rang and rang. Velvert was near tears, and said, "Here, *listen*." He gave it to Zeke, and Zeke listened to it ring, and he handed it to the next guy, and the next guy listened to it ring. He handed it to me, and it rang half a ring...and then Jimi picked up. I knew it was Jimi because of the sound of his voice. He said something like, "Hey man, what's happening. Who is this?" And I stood up, and said, "Oh, this is Velvert, Jimi." I handed it to him, and he went off in the corner – whispering and talking to Jimi.

It was the same day I first saw him, because Velvert came back and said, "Jimi's playing tonight, and he said I can bring somebody with me." Everybody clamored to go, and I didn't. He said, "*You!*" And he was pointing at me. So, we became really, really close friends – in my middle teenage years there. We went to a lot of shows. Jimi could get you into anywhere if you went along with him. So, somewhere along the line – it might have been at the Fillmore East, where I first actually met him. In other words, I was part of his entourage. Velvert went to school in Brooklyn, and we went to school in Manhattan. So, I would have never met him except for that odd event at my friend Zeke's house.

I didn't say anything to Jimi [the first time Richard met Jimi] so there isn't anything to report. I was just in the room – he was getting ready to go on stage, and mostly afterwards. I remember once going without Velvert to someplace in Midtown Manhattan, and I went to this stage door, and Jimi hadn't arrived yet. And his manager – I didn't know it was his manager at the time – was in the middle of the street, jumping up and down, literally pulling the hair out of his head, saying, "Where is he?! Where is he?! I'll fucking kill him!" And Jimi drove up in one of his Corvettes. The guy opened up the driver's side door…and *manhandled* Jimi.

He pulled him out, and lifted him up by the scruff of the neck, and said, "You'll never do that to me again when you know you have a show to do!" I was talking to some of Jimi's friends – some black girls, Esmeralda and Evan – and I said, "Who was that?" And they said. "You don't want to know…*that was Jimi's manager*." He was a gangster. After the shows, we would go backstage, and there would be other people backstage, that knew him on a more personal level. I mean, I was just an onlooker, really. And I tended not to say anything, so I'd last longer. Because if a 16-year-old kid starts talking, somebody's going to escort them out of the room.

Didn't you once have a surprisingly violent confrontation with Jimi?

At the Salvation – a mob-run club in Greenwich Village. And he was advertising it as a "small, semi-private show." I still have the ticket. It was like ten

bucks – it was "Black Roman Orgy: Music by
Hendrix, Gypsy Sun and Rainbows." So, I arrived,
and I was waiting for Velvert, but he was late, so I
went down by myself. I ended up sitting at the same
table as Jimi – a big, round table. The music had
stopped – he had apparently gotten the wrong kind of
feedback. They hadn't set up the public address
system properly. So, he was frustrated. And then we
were all drinking. At the time, he was fond of Mateus
and Lancers – these are sparkling Rose wines. So, we
were all pretty smashed.

    And the guy next to Jimi got up and went to
the bathroom, and I got pushed – so I was sitting on
Jimi's left side, right next to him. And he started
talking to me, saying all this sort of cartoon-esque
hyperbole. Like, "Hey man, the rings of Saturn are
blah blah, woof woof." One of his favorite ways of
finishing a sentence when he couldn't think of the
words to say would be, "Blah blah, woof woof." So,
anyway, I wasn't saying anything, and he was talking
to I think Billy Cox – who was sitting on his right
side. And then he would talk to me.

    And he was like, *really* downtrodden. Super-
sad. He was talking about, "I'm not long for the
world." And "I'm being made to be like a clown. I'm
in the circus and I can't get out." Finally, I broke my
silence, and said, "Jimi, you should be able to do
whatever you want to do. People really love you and
what you do." And I guess he took that part and
parcel of the bullshit he was hearing, because he
called it, "Mickey Mouse" – which apparently is a
term used in the army for "bullshit." Like what the
sergeant says or the drill sergeant.

    Anyway, the time came to leave – the lights

came on, and everybody groaned. The closing time was 4am. So, we got up and pushed the table out, and I put on my jacket – it was November, so it was really chilly outside. And Jimi put on his coat facing away from me, swung around, and struck me – three times – with his fists. In the face, the stomach, and the face – like a left, right, left. And all I did was sit down and think, "Oh…he packs a pretty good punch for a scrawny black guy." And then I heard people saying, "Jimi's in a fight! Somebody's trying to kill Jimi! We'll kill him!" And I knew they were talking about me – so I sat there until everybody had left. Literally, *everybody* – except for the janitor, who told me, "You've got to leave now. I've got to lock up." So, I trepidatiously left, and walked up the stairs because it was in a basement.

And Jimi was waiting for me in his Corvette – in the parking lot which was opposite the club. He rolled down his window, and crooked his finger, like, "Come over here." So, I went over, and he took my hands and started crying, saying, "I'm sorry, man. I'm so sorry." And I'm going, "Jimi, it's OK. Go and get some rest." But my attitude was that it had imparted a measure of his strength to me. And my intention was to absorb it. Like Chinese kung fu fighters, y'know? They will steal the energy from their opponent. So, when he punched me, it didn't knock me out or anything – I just sat down, and I thought, "*Interesting.*"

But then later on, he cried on my hands, and rubbed the tears on. I was like, "Come on Jimi…go home and go to sleep." I guess he knew that I was in the entourage – he knew that I was Velvert's best friend – and was really apologetic. And then he finally rolled up the window and drove away, and Velvert popped up from behind, because he was hiding in the doorway – he had watched the whole thing. And he had been talking to Jimi before I came up and out, and I guess Jimi was like, "I punched one of your friends. I'm so sorry." That was my "big communication" with Jimi.

And after that, I got to go into the studio with him. What they would do is be at the Record Plant, and they would allow people in the control room, as they listened to yesterday's take. So, I heard a version of "Izabella" – actually backwards. And Jimi talked to the engineer, and said, "I want to do a song where you have four bars forward and four bars backward, four bars forward and four bars backward, eight bars forward and four bars backward." And the engineer, Gary Kellgren, I think, he dropped his head, and said, "Jimi, that's impossible. It would take *a year*."

Because back then, we were dealing with tape – and you'd have to cut the tape a zillion times, turn the pieces around. But what they do in the studio when you're working with tape, is you store them with the tail out. In other words, you would play them, and then you keep fast-forwarding until you get to the end, and you store them that way. So when you want to work on them, you've got to rewind the whole tape. But Jimi said no – he wanted to hear it backwards. You just turn the tape over and put it in the feed reel, so, we listened to "Izabella" backwards – for about eight minutes or so. Then, when they were about to get to work, they would politely ask people to leave.

Where else would Jimi hang out?

The one that I know the most about is Steve Paul's Scene because we used to go there and get in underage. It was a little club in a basement on 46th Street in Manhattan. One time we went down to see Buddy Guy, and John Hammond Jr. was opening for him. And then Jimi came down later – but we had already left, because of something that happened. Velvert had broken a string on Buddy's guitar, and he had put on a string that he had found in a guitar case there, but he put it on backwards. What I mean to say is when you turn the tuning pegs – which he had learned from Jimi – he turned the peg the wrong way, and he was afraid that Buddy would kill him.

His manager said, "You all better be careful with that. *Buddy's got a gun and he's not afraid to use it.*" I wanted to stay, but Velvert wanted to leave – he was scared to death. So, my friendship with him was more important than one night at Steve Paul's Scene – so I missed it when Jimi came in. He used to go there *a lot* and play with whoever was playing there. He liked to jam. He used to go to a place called Ungano's. Mostly small clubs – not theater gigs. Every night – he was a night bird…and back then, I was, too.

Didn't you also attend Woodstock?

I went to Woodstock and I didn't sleep the whole time – *without drugs*. Just from the sheer energy of it. I left halfway through [Jimi's set] – I thought it was sad and pathetic. I mean, in hindsight knowing what the circumstances were, it was just from fatigue and being tired. They made him wait overnight to play – and he was ready to play at 8pm or 11pm. And they made him wait until the next sunrise.

I didn't like that band [Gypsy Sun and Rainbows] very much. I liked the Band of Gypsys' performances at the Fillmore – they were awfully great. But conga players…it was all a bit ragged. So, I left halfway through. I believe that was the last time I saw Jimi perform.

Was Jimi giving just Velvert guitar lessons, or both of you?

Just Velvert. But I lived four or five blocks from Jimi's house. So, Velvert would leave Jimi's, and he would want to come over to my house, because he knew I had a guitar, and he would come over right afterwards, and we would practice the guitar – trading the guitar back and forth, between us. And he was showing me all this stuff that Jimi was showing him. Some of it got in, and some of it didn't – over the years. But, I remember what we were doing. It was second-hand lessons. Not first-hand. Jimi didn't have any guitar students – besides Velvert. And Velvert was like his little brother. He really had his arm around Velvert.

Of course. [In response to being asked if anything stuck with him that Velvert showed him] But how can I describe them? These are physical things you do on the guitar. But yes, I remember some of them. Some of them I can play, and some of them I remember, but I can't address with my hands. Absolutely not. [In response to being asked if any of these techniques showed up in Television songs]

Did you see Jimi again?

I saw him a couple of times in the studio, and then we got separated. My parents moved to New Jersey, and they gave me a choice – "You can move to New Jersey or you can stay in Manhattan on your own." So, I moved to New Jersey with them. And that was kind of the end of that period of my life. Then, I heard he died and it was quite a shock. But considering what he had told me, it wasn't a shock. Because what he was saying to me in Salvation was, "I'm not long for the world" and "They got me on a string" and "They're parading me around like a puppet and I can't do what I want." Stuff like that. So, when he died, it was like, "Oh…*everything he said was true*."

Where did you say Jimi's apartment was?

On 12th Street between 5th and 6th Avenues. On the north side of the street. I don't remember the number of the address. It's a tall building – *a lot* of apartments.

Why was Jimi so upset?

I heard things not from Jimi himself but from other people like Velvert, who told me about a meeting Jimi had with his manager, and Jimi was asking him to cancel a concert tour – because he was tired. He was fatigued and wanted to work on new stuff in the studio.

And the manager said, "Listen Jimi, do you like your little fingers? Do you like playing your little guitar? Because if you do, you'll do *exactly* as I say.

There's a great deal of money to be made here, Jimi. And someday, one day, you'll be worth more to me dead than alive, Jimi. And that day will come."

So, it was a pretty boldfaced threat. And it turned out to be true – he had drowned in wine. They forced wine down, and he had wine in his lungs. That's murder.

Was it murder, suicide, or an accident?

Murder. Considering all the evidence and the things I heard – it was distinctly murder.

Did you keep in contact with Velvert after moving to New Jersey?

For a little while, then I didn't, then he moved to Los Angeles, then I went to Los Angeles and saw him a little bit, and then surprisingly, we got back in touch with each other shortly before he died, and tried to re-establish our friendship – and then he passed away [on December 11, 2000, at the age of 49]. I went to his funeral and spoke to his mom and the other people that were there – Eddie Kramer was there.

What did you think of Velvert's album [1972's *The Velvert Turner Group*]?

I thought it was so-so. He didn't write any of the songs on it. The bass player did a lot of the songs – he ended up being in the Knack. So he got success – Prescott Niles. But it was disappointing to me – although I liked the first song, "Madonna (Of the Seven Moons)." But Velvert did not have what Jimi had.

I mean, he could play Jimi's stuff and he could play his own stuff with that…you could definitely tell he studied with Hendrix, rather than *study* Hendrix. And it shows in his guitar playing. But Velvert always told me, "When you play, it sounds backwards to me." That is what he got out of my playing. [Laughs]

You released an all-Jimi covers album in 2009, *The Jamie Neverts Story*.

We would be hanging out with the kids after school and we would want to go visit Jimi. And Velvert said, "We can't say we're going to go visit Hendrix, or else the entire crowd will follow us." So, we invented the name "Jamie Neverts" as a pseudonym for Jimi. At one point, I thought, "I should really do a tribute to Velvert and to Jimi and to what I learned back then." It mostly concentrates on songs from his first and second records – the shorter songs that Chas had produced.

I had a segue that went "Axis: Bold as Love" into "Are You Experienced," but his family wouldn't let me put it out as a single track – they made me fade the middle and fade in the other song. I had a hell of a time getting permission to put it out. And I couldn't use Jimi's name on it – *anywhere*. And because it didn't mention Jimi anywhere on it, it's *The Jamie Neverts Story* – some weird title – it didn't end up selling very well. But it's in my catalog – so there it is. And I had an enormous amount of fun doing it.

Lastly, how would you describe Jimi's personality?

He was shy and he was wonderful and congenial and pleasant. There was nothing to speak of that was egotistical. He was not ego-driven as far as I knew. Aside from when he got drunk and would lash out – because he *was* in a tough situation. He couldn't do what he wanted. And so, that affected him, certainly. He wrote "Manic Depression" – which is bipolar. And I supposed he might have had some of that. But I thought he was a wonderful man.

Chapter 19
Woodstock

An interview I conducted with Billy Cox about Woodstock (and other subjects), which appeared in the September 2005 issue of Guitarist.

Jimi Hendrix
Freedom!

Woodstock remembered by Hendrix's bassman in Gypsy Sun & Rainbows, Billy Cox...

What do you remember about the whole Woodstock experience?

It was great. We rehearsed, had a house in Woodstock for maybe 30 days, and then the Woodstock Festival finally came up. We worked, practiced and rehearsed very diligently for that. And the day finally came when we did that, and it was kind of a relief off our minds. We really did it as a group. One cannot separate the music from the festival itself, for they both were magical. The people and the entertainers co-existed in the spirit of oneness. I consider myself blessed to have played at the party of the millennium. The jury is still out on [the DVD *Live at Woodstock*], I have not heard it, did not have anything to do with the production.

But I know what I was a part of on stage, and that was good music. At Woodstock, Jerry Velez, Juma Edwards [also known as Juma Sultan], Larry Lee, Mitch Mitchell, Jimi Hendrix, and Billy Cox were on stage close to two hours. The group was tight because we were well rehearsed, and we were all on the same vibe. "Jam Back at the House" showcases a cohesiveness of the group. At Woodstock, Jimi and I knew we were witnessing his "Sky Church concept." Sky Church was a vision that Jimi had shared with me when we first reunited in New York.

Right here, I'm going to give you a little musical trivia – I'm the only bandmate that can say he played with the Jimi Hendrix Experience, Band of Gypsys, and at Woodstock, it was Gypsy, Sun and Rainbows. The music Gypsy, Sun and Rainbows made at Woodstock is standing right now the test of time.

What was Jimi's impression of Woodstock?

He thought we did real well. In fact, he was so into it, if you listen closely to "The Star-Spangled Banner," you will see that I stayed on him. We had a vibe of our own, and I knew that I had to lock in with him mentally. And when he started "The Star-Spangled Banner," that impromptu thing, you hear the first four, five, or six notes; I'm in there with him. Then I said, "Wait a minute, we didn't rehearse this, and it doesn't sound too good with me playing." I backed away, and he continued and made a classic out of that.

What do you remember about hearing his version for the first time?

It was great – it was him releasing himself. His freedom had finally been unleashed.

207 WOODSTOCK

How would you describe the vibe at Woodstock and the audience?

Great – we went and played with the attitude of, "Look at all those people, everybody's doing something different." It's like watching television; we'll go with the vibe. So the energy from them came to us, and we threw it right back at them.

How do you feel Jimi's performance at Woodstock compares to his other famous live shows (Monterey, New Year's '70, etc.)?

It's right in the cut. He was very good – excellent.

What do you think Jimi's attitude to playing live was at the time?

In the earlier times, when he was with Noel and Mitch, the songs were very simple songs – "Foxy Lady" [hums riff], "Purple Haze" [hums riff]. The songs were very simple in their formation and in their production. And then, he was growing musically, and all artists do grow. The body grows – new cells come every day. So all artists continue to grow in some way, form, or fashion – whether they're a painter, a musician, whatever. So he was growing. The simplicity of the "Foxy Ladys" and the "Purple Hazes" now went into some pretty intricate things, like "Jam Back at the House" and then later the "Freedoms," the "Dolly Daggers," and "In from the Storm." And you don't have the time to do a lot of pyrotechnics; you've got to play.

Why didn't the Gypsy Sun and Rainbows line-up ever do an album?

There were a lot of, I'll say "entities," that never wanted that group to go any further. They felt that they started off with the concept of Mitch and Noel, let's continue that. This was just a whim from Jimi, get it over with, and let's go back to the original concept. But you can't go back home.

But Jimi did want to take 'Gypsy Sun and Rainbows' into the studio to make an album though?

Yeah, he wanted to do some other things. It was stopped cold.

How would you compare playing with Gypsy Sun and Rainbows to Band of Gypsys?

It was just a different thing. We had a different drummer, went in a different direction, did some different things. Like people ask me, "Do you like playing with Buddy Miles or do you like playing with Mitch Mitchell?" I like playing with good musicians who know their act. So Buddy's good, Mitch is good. I have no problems with them. We had six musicians on stage at Woodstock, and we had three on stage at the Fillmore East, so there's a difference there.

Talk a bit about the Cort Freedom bass.

They asked me to do a bass. All musicians want to

do something different for instruments if they had the opportunity. So I came up with the concept 15, 20 years ago. I put it down in some file cabinets and left it there. I was approached, and I said, "Oh, I've got some stuff." Sent the drawings in, they said, "OK, we did about three or four basses." Prototype, prototype, prototype, and then finally, "Ah, this is the one." I like it, I play it every day I play. If nobody else likes it, that's too bad – but I'm enjoying it.

What are some memories of being in the military with Jimi (in the early 60's)?

I first met him; we formed a group there. I felt intuitively he was unique. We became friends, and that friendship lasted a lifetime.

How would you describe Jimi as a person when you first met him, and when he became a rock star?

When I met him, he was ten years younger – when you grow, you mature. He was a little more mature.

Was it true Jimi invited you to go with him to England when he first went over in 1966, to play in his band?

Yes. He called me and said, "Hey Billy, this guy's going to send me over to Europe to make me a star." He was in New York, and he said, "I've told him about you, you can go, too." I said, "Well Jimi, I don't even have any fare to get to New York. Number two, I'm renting an amp. Number three, I've got three strings on my bass" – the fourth was tied in a square knot. And he said, "Well that's OK – I'll make it and we'll get together. I'll send for you." And that was it.

What was your last conversation with Jimi?

"Hey man, we're going back in the studio Friday, OK? *Be there.*"

Chapter 20
Monika

According to former Scorpions guitarist
Uli Jon Roth, one of Jimi's last girlfriends,
Monika Dannemann, knew "the real Jimi."

ULI JON ROTH: I began to understand a lot more about Jimi particularly after I met Monika Dannemann. Because Jimi had taught her an awful lot about what his songs meant and his messages. And it was *she* who gave me the key to understanding really his more spiritual message. That would be too long to do [explain some of the messages Jimi explained to Monika]. And I don't really want to pick out any highlights.

But in general, she was one of the very few persons around Jimi who *really* understood what he was all about, and he sensed that – that's why he shared an awful lot with her. And normally, he didn't – he was very private in those things. Only very few people, like Billy Cox for instance, would know about his more spiritual things, that were an extremely important part for him, and kind of like a driving force.

But yes, she was a kindred spirit, and I believe was his soul mate. They were quite similar in some respects – although totally different in others. It was obvious when I got to meet her, how much she really understood – and she understood more than other people. And that's reflected in the quality of her paintings. And he made her do these paintings, because when they first met, she was just an amateur – having done some portraits, and her talent was obvious. He saw them and said, "You should be an artist...a painter. Because you've got what it takes." Eventually, he said, "I want you to compliment my message with the paintings." When you look at the paintings, it's borne out by the quality.

In fact, I remember a couple of days after Monika died [on April 5, 1996, at the age of 50], I got a phone call from Mitch Mitchell, who said, "Look, I'd just seen Monika's book [1995's *The Inner World of Jimi Hendrix*], and she was totally in tune with Jimi." He saw the quality and he saw all that, and that was nice to know, because I liked Mitch. It was really a nice thing for him to do. But anyways, it's like a raw subject. It's not easy to talk about, because there are so many different angles and facets.

And of course, so much has been written about Jimi in the past, and a lot of it is either untrue or largely distorted. Sometimes, by people who say things maybe with good intentions, but with a blurred memory. And some are by people who just want to make themselves look good – they twist the truth in whatever angle is needed at the moment. So, don't take everything at face value that you see and read about Jimi. There are some sources that are much better than others. Like Leon Hendrix [Jimi's brother] – he knew Jimi and grew up with Jimi in the early days, and he'll tell you what it was like.

In fact, talking about Leon, we were in Seattle just the day before yesterday, and a friend of mine invited me to come on a guided tour to a Hendrix exhibit at the newly coined Jimi Hendrix Park. It was really interesting, because they have a lot of Jimi's early watercolors, and I knew Jimi was gifted visually. *Extremely* gifted. But when I saw those, there were several that I had never seen, and they really struck home.

There as a twelve-year-old kid, with the talent to become a great painter and great artist, because he had it down. He had the composition, he had the colors, he had very talented strokes as a draftsman and an artist. I know about these things because I studied these things, and then I do oil paintings myself. So, I was blown away by his perception and .depth, and also, typically, he created his own style – even as a twelve-year-old, when drawing a painting. And he used to do so many. Leon said he was always at it.

That's a side of Jimi that is not that much known about, but it's part of the whole picture. He was such a visually gifted artist, and the visual element comes through in all of his guitar work. When you listen to "Voodoo Chile" the slow version or "Slight Return," the guitar – although pentatonic in technical terms – is just complete sound paintings. He used to sit at the ocean and look at the waves coming in and the surfers, and study the way it flowed, and then, he would emulate that in the swirls of his guitar playing – speeding up and down a lick. Which is a rubato kind of technique, which normally you find in classic guitar players or in classic compositions – but not in somebody that plays rock.

Hendrix did that all the time, because he played with time – he was a rhythmical genius. He would sometimes speed up and slow down deliberately – just like in his real life. And then, be right on the beat again – creating enormous amounts of tension in the process. That's very different from normal blues players, who would just play the lick as it's written in the pocket, but not with that extra special visual dimension – that Hendrix always had in everything he did.

FRANCIS BUCHHOLZ [Scorpions bassist]: "We'll Burn the Sky" [a Scorpions tune off 1977's *Taken By Force*] is a favorite song of mine. First of all, the lyrics were written by Uli Roth's girlfriend, who was the ex-friend of Jimi Hendrix [Monika Dannemann]. It's about burning the sky because things are not as they should be – that is my interpretation. I like the rhythm, I like the bass, and it always went down good with the audience. We played it a long time with the Scorpions. It's a great live song.*

ULI JON ROTH: It's obvious – it was about Jimi.*

*Both quotes are from the 2016 book, *German Metal Machine: Scorpions in the '70s*, by Greg Prato.

Chapter 21
Electric Lady

An article I penned for the September/October 1998 issue of Experience Hendrix, *for which Eddie Kramer was interviewed.*

JIMI'S GIRL
ELECTRIC LADY STUDIOS:
HENDRIX'S LABOR OF LOVE

Picture this...you're one of the world's biggest recording stars, and your tours are instant sellouts. You've purchased one of your favorite nightclubs, which is being renovated into a beautiful recording studio. Things should be going smoothly, right? If you were Jimi Hendrix from 1968 through 1970, not exactly.

Hendrix's manager, Michael Jeffery, had Hendrix working at a breakneck pace, and a few unfavorable business matters early in his career eventually hamstrung his finances. But despite all the distractions and hardships, Electric Lady Studios emerged in 1970 as one of the most cutting-edge (and popular) studios of its time.

Due to his hectic recording and touring schedule, Hendrix didn't have much say in the studio's construction, but one man who was a major force in its conception was producer/engineer Eddie Kramer, who oversaw the whole process from beginning to end.

Kramer took some time out recently to discuss the creation of Electric Lady, and explain what put it ahead of the pack.

Kramer began his career as an independent engineer, overseeing many of the Hendrix albums released during Hendrix's lifetime, plus several posthumous collections. "That whole era was one of big change for a lot of people," he says. "Becoming an independent engineer was a scary moment, but it seemed to work out well. I did two big things: Led Zeppelin and Woodstock."

In 1968, Hendrix stumbled upon a funky New York City joint called the Generation Club, on West 8th Street in Greenwich Village. Enchanted by the atmosphere there, he began jamming at a few late night sessions and later decided that he wanted to own it. "Jimi decided to buy it with Michael Jeffery," says Kramer, "and I think it was halfway through '69 that I got a phone call from Jim Marron, who was the maître d' at the Scene Club, which was where Jimi used to go jam a lot. Michael had hired Jim Marron away from there to become the manager of this new Generation Club."

"So they said, 'Jimi and Michael want you to come down and take a look at the club. They want to put a small recording studio in the corner, to tape just live stuff.' And I went down to look at it and went, 'You guys are out of your minds! Forget the nightclub, let's make this the best god-damned studio in the world'!"

Hendrix loved the idea and the seeds of what would eventually become Electric Lady were planted. Looking back, Kramer admits he was surprised that they were so receptive to this idea: "It was a bit of a shock because John Storyk, who was the architect, had already designed a nightclub for them. And they picked him because he had designed a weird kind of club; it was a whole different kind of atmospheric turn-on club. It was all on different levels, lots of drapes, it was a very weird thing. It actually made the centerpiece of *LIFE Magazine* for that year." Storyk was understandably upset when he found out that the plans he'd worked so hard on had been changed, but he remained on board to design Electric Lady.

At the time, few recording studios catered to rock bands; most were designed years before, solely for recording classical music. This posed a problem for artists like Hendrix, and Kramer was committed to correcting this.

"Most studios up to that point were boxes, very antiseptic, with not much attention paid to the acoustics," he explains. "We tried to make it a womb-like place, a warm, comforting place, so that when Jimi walked in there, he'd feel incredibly happy. Like the white carpets on the wall [which are still in existence today], and if you look up at the ceiling, there's a complete theatre lighting system. Its function was to wash the walls in different colors, so Jimi would say one night, 'Hey man, I want purple' and we would dial in the colors for him and he'd go, 'Oh wow, this is cool.' It was an artist-driven studio."

Soon after plans were drawn up, says Kramer, Hendrix offered his sole request for the project: "Jimi said to me, 'Hey man, I'm only gonna ask you for one thing, and that's round windows.' And I was like, 'Uhhh, OK Jimi!' In fact, still to this day, you can see the round windows on some of the doors."

With Hendrix unavailable to oversee its planning and construction, Storyk and Kramer began creating Jimi's dream studio on their own, with the two assigning themselves specific duties. "What John Storyk and I came up with was an advanced studio," says Kramer. "He came up with the shapes and the concept of the design, and I came up with the design for the console and all the electronics that went in there."

Hendrix made it a point to stay away from the studio while it was being built, placing absolute trust in Kramer and Storyk. When he finally saw the near-completed facility, Hendrix was happy that he had trusted his instincts. "He was really, really happy with that studio," says Kramer. "When he finally came down to work in the studio, he was just completely knocked out and didn't want to leave. He was there every day and every night for like four months, from May to August. He was there literally as much as he could be."

Although many were taken by Electric Lady's looks, it was the recording equipment that truly set it apart from its competitors. "Technologically, we wanted to make it as advanced as we could," says Kramer. "We designed the board so that it was capable of going to 24 tracks, because we saw that was coming up. You know, 16 track was already in for about a year. But the console was designed for 24, and one of the main tape machines in Studio A was wired for 24. We had 16 tracks of Dolby and every piece of outboard gear we could think of – from equalizers to the earliest digital delays. When people walked in there, [they] saw how it was built and how it felt and what the vibe was. Everybody was really knocked out."

"You were knocked out for two reasons; one

was aesthetically – it was very beautiful. And technologically it was very cutting edge. Also, acoustically, it sounded fabulous. When people came in to cut tracks they walk away saying, 'Wow, this studio sounds great.' The whole design was just so far ahead of its time when compared to anything that had been built, with its curved ceiling, hidden lights, the 24-track console and tape machine, all the outboard gear, the acoustics of the room."

But Electric Lady's construction did have its setbacks. Several permits had to be acquired first, and then a torrential downpour that lasted several days flooded the studio's site. Plus, sump pumps and extra soundproofing were required when it was discovered that Electric Lady was located on a tributary of the underground Minetta Creek. Additionally, Kramer ran into some problems with the builders of the studio's consoles.

"The guys who were building the console ripped us off," he says. "They would show us the console for Studio A, and then the next week would show us the Studio B console, but they were taking the parts form A and moving them to the B console! It was terrible. We had to go in one day with a big truck and remove all the parts for both consoles, their test equipment and everything from this guy. He was a complete rip-off artist, and the sheriff was going to close him down, but we went up with a truck, and a bunch of guys took everything. Shimon Ron [the chief maintenance engineer] had to rebuild the Studio A console and completely build the Studio B console from scratch. It was just a nightmare."

Since Electric Lady wasn't completed at the time of Hendrix's death [Studio A was the only functioning studio], it was hard for Kramer and company to carry on and complete what would have been Jimi's home away from home. Kramer explains, "When he died, we all immediately thought, 'Oh my God, what is going to happen to the studio?' And somehow or other, we just got ourselves together and said, 'Look, this is not going to stop us. We have to keep going, Jimi would have wanted us to keep going.' And we picked up the pieces."

What they ended up creating was a studio that is synonymous with Jimi Hendrix, a studio with a great deal of attention paid to detail. Of course, it would have been sweeter if Hendrix had been there for its completion, but the short amount of time that Hendrix spent there had rubbed off. "He left behind such an incredible vibe and such a great legacy," says Kramer. "Everybody worshipped that place; it's a monument to his genius and his creativity. And it continues. Everybody who comes into that studio feels his vibe. Whether it's psychological or actual, it doesn't matter. It's a very important place."

Indeed it is, and will always be.

Chapter 22
Isle Of Wight

An article I penned that appeared in Classic Rock's The Great Rock Festivals Special Issue *from 2008.*

"We Want the World, and We Want it Now" –
The 1970 Isle of Wight Festival

They thought it was going to be several days of peace, love, and music – just like Woodstock had been a year earlier. They thought wrong. Marred by poor planning and audience unrest, the 1970 Isle of Wight Festival turned out to be a precursor of sorts to what was to follow in the coming decade. Several members of bands that played the festival, as well as director Murray Lerner (who filmed most of the acts), look back on the good, the bad, and the ugly.

You could make a valid argument that the '60s were all about trying to change the world, and that the '70s were all about the individual. Perhaps Jim Morrison summed it up best while performing with the Doors at the 1970 Isle of Wight Festival – "We want the world, and we want it now!"

"First of all, a huge crowd – potentially dangerous, but never became that way," recalls film maker Murray Lerner about the festival. "A lot of hassle between the songs, but then when the songs came, things quieted down. And some great classic rock performances, like the Who, Hendrix, and the Doors. Joni Mitchell was more in the folk tradition, but she was great, and Miles Davis, of course."

Heckling the performers, crowds breaking

down fences and getting in for free, anarchists disrupting the proceedings, a fire on top of the stage, and festival organizers being in well over their head were just some of the "highlights" of the 1970 Isle of Wight Festival. As a result, there wouldn't be another Isle of Wight Festival for another 32 years.

The inaugural Isle of Wight Festival occurred in 1968, supposedly when the Isle of Wight Swimming Pool Association needed to raise money. The idea of holding a pop festival sounded like a splendid idea, and a one hundred acre field, Hayles Field (dubbed "Hells Field"), was secured as the site. Held over two days, 10,000 attendees were treated to sets by such artists as the Move, Tyrannosaurus Rex, Jefferson Airplane, and Arthur Brown, among others.

The '68 festival was such a success that its founders/organizers, the Foulk brothers (Ray, Ron, and Bill) and Rikki Farr, set their sights on putting together another festival. And this time, they planned big. Able to convince Bob Dylan to come out of his "exile" to play his first show in a dog's age, the 1969 Isle of Wight Festival was held at Forelands Farm, Wootton, and attracted 100,000 music fans.

And this time, the crowd was treated to three days of music – including the Who, the Moody Blues, and the Band (both on their own and backing Dylan), while spectators included various members of the Rolling Stones, the Beatles, and Pink Floyd, as well as Elton John.

With the festival growing by leaps and bounds between its first two years, there was no way anyone could have predicted the amount of people that would turn up for the 1970 edition. Now stretched over five days, the festival featured some of the world's biggest music names – Jimi Hendrix, the Doors, and the Who, to name but a few.

Sensing that the audience would be even larger than the previous years, a new festival site was scouted. And the organizers thought they'd found a keeper at Churchill's Farm in Calbourne. But when they were unable to secure it (allegedly because a member of the city council expected a "cut" of the earnings), it was determined that the 1970 Isle of Wight Festival would be held at Afton Farm. Only one small problem – it was overlooked by Afton Down, a hill that created a perfect view of the stage. Despite knowing that there would be a large number of non-paying patrons camping out on the hill rather than paying for entry, the Festival went ahead.

Director Murray Lerner was no stranger to filming music festivals, as he had directed the Academy Award nominated 1967 film, *Festival!*, which chronicled the highlights from several years of the Newport Folk Festival in the US – which included Bob Dylan's first ever "electric" performance. By 1970, Lerner was ready to document another music festival on film, and hooked up with the Isle of Wight.

"It was bigger than Woodstock, it had 600,000 people," explains Lerner. "Dylan was there the year before – he put it on the map. They had 150,000 people at that time. But because he had been there, it got a lot of attention, and became a big deal. You might actually call the film *Bob Dylan Once Sang Here.* [Laughs] I'm serious, because the fringe element – the kids that said they didn't have money to sleep anywhere or do anything – that was called desolation row, after his song 'Desolation Row.' [It] became the byword of the fringe element, which was not such a fringe element – it was hundreds of thousands of people. Huge. You see it in the aerials if you saw the film."

But almost immediately after he began filming, Lerner discovered an unexpected "vibe" surrounding the 1970 festival. "I think that whole movement began to break apart. It started with the Newport stuff, and then became commercialized, and the kids got upset about the commercialization and the money part that was going on in terms of co-opting the music. So there was a lot of 'back-and-forth.' And then they were radicalized by...I guess a certain element went to radicalize these kids. To get these kids to think about what's wrong with society essentially. When you get that many people, and one guy starts 'Let's get in for nothing,' there's a ripple effect. So they all want to get in – smashing the fences."

Lerner also recalls "A lot of trouble in terms of the crowd. There were no fatalities, unlike some other places. Then there was the potential fire which we show [in the film], but it was just a guy was told two weeks earlier to schedule fireworks. And without thinking, he just shot them off, and everyone thought, 'OK, the stage is being attacked by flame' [Laughs]. I thought that was 'it'."

As with most multi-day long festivals, the first two days – 26 August and 27 August (a Wednesday and a Thursday) – featured mostly newer artists, as a sort of warm up to the bigger acts that were to follow. Included were performances by such then up-and-comers as Supertramp and Terry Reid.

Lerner remembers the first days featuring artists that were embraced, and also rejected, by the still-assembling crowd.

"David Bromberg received a phenomenal reception from the audience. It was funny because he thought that they were booing him. They weren't – they were cheering him. When he got off the stage, he said, 'I'm a star!' You would've thought that Bromberg was going to be the biggest star in the world that night. I think he had four encores."

Unfortunately, a then-unknown Kris Kristofferson didn't fare nearly as well. "He had a lot of difficulties with the audience. I think just because his voice was lower than most were used to, and there was a lot of catcalls. He said, 'I guess we'll finish, providing we're not shot.' Then he walked off the stage without taking a bow or anything. But on the other hand, it kind of set the stage for his fame. Because a guy who was really important at the festival became his manager, and built him up right after that. He became not only a singing star, but a movie star."

When Friday, 28 August rolled around, the festival was truly gaining steam, and quickly reaching its peak attendance figure, said to be 600,000.

One of the first true standout performances of the '70 Festival came on this day – Chicago. Although they later became known as power balladeers in the '80s, Chicago early on was much more rock-based (led by the late/great guitarist Terry Kath), with a blazing horn section that made them stand out from the pack. Chicago's sax player, Walter Parazaider, recalls the events leading up to their set.

"They had us in a holding area on another island, with cottages and everything, which was just spectacular. The weather was great. Isle of Wight was our first experience at [playing festivals]. And you talk about people being really young – eyes as big as silver dollars, and taking everything in. From the campers backstage – the people that were the modern day gypsies. My wife and I were just walking around, taking in the whole backstage area – that was a show within itself. I just remember walking by different people that were from Austria, Germany, or whatever. I thought of the old *Dracula* or *Wolfman* movies, where there was a gypsy cart. I remember sitting with a bunch of people, and realizing they were gypsies. There were areas back there where you could warm up."

Parazaider also remembers being overwhelmed by the event. "The whole spectacle of it was amazing. It was massive. And when you get that amount of people – just a whisper from a crowd like that is a roar. It's an unbelievable thing. And if you don't keep within yourself, you could just as easily throw your horn in the crowd and run around like a lunatic just freaking out from it."

But Parazaider and his band mates needn't have worried, as they were warmly received by the crowd. "The crowd was very receptive, and it was very receptive from the start. We wondered, but that first album [1969's *Chicago Transit Authority*] had 'I'm A Man' on it – a cover of a Spencer Davis tune – and it had gone over quite well in England. They knew the material and we were quite well received."

"It was one of the highlights of our career – it

was a knockout. To play in front of 600,000 people – at that point in our career, we were nuts. We were just sky high from the whole experience before we even hit the stage, and had to really keep our feet on the ground, and pay attention to our business, which was the music. We all sort of hung together, I don't want to say spiritually, but we were all close in the original band. On stage, we just sort of hung together to keep ourselves together to survive a maelstrom – like 600,000 people yelling. To compare that to any other shows, at that time, it was the epitome of anything we had done."

Later the same day, the crowd was treated to further sets by Procol Harum and the Voices of East Harlem, before the day ended in the wee hours of the morning, with a set by hard blues rockers Cactus. Cactus' drummer, Carmine Appice, recalls that the festival's main attraction for many, Jimi Hendrix, had turned up early to hang out. "The thing that I remember the most is the fact that we were hanging out a lot backstage with Hendrix. It had sort of a 'tent' kind of vibe – everybody had little areas where they hung out. Hendrix was hanging out with us – he and Jim McCarty [Cactus' guitarist] were real close. And we knew Hendrix for a long time – I knew Jimi since '65, before he was even 'Jimi Hendrix'."

"I remember a lot of jamming going on, with two guitars and banging on tabletops. It's too long ago to remember conversations. At these festivals, there was always a lot of drugs. We used to drink a sip of wine backstage, and you didn't know – sometimes it would have mescaline in it or something weird. Everybody's pot smoking. It was a pretty fun backstage area. That's the thing I remember most about it. It wasn't like the best of circumstances, as far as the backstage areas. From what I remember, it was some sort of tent area."

Appice remembers that the weather had taken a turn for the worst during their set. "It was cold – it was rainy. I think it was damp and foggy. Horrible. I don't remember it as being a tremendous show. I think the Isle of Wight was a bit of a disaster. And that was the drag of being a headliner of those kind of festivals, because that used to happen to us with Vanilla Fudge when he headlined some festivals. By the time you go on, it's like the wee hours of the morning, and your audience is going away. I mean, you look at Hendrix playing Woodstock – he had nobody there. It became such a legendary performance, but nobody was there, which is pretty funny. He played to an empty house, whereas Santana played when the place was packed. It was the same kind of thing here, but I don't think they had a lot of people. I might be wrong, but it didn't stand out – the performance – in my head."

Appice also recalls the growing unrest among audience members that led to an indifferent reaction. "I remember something about that. But maybe that would account on why it didn't leave an impression as far as the audience – maybe the audience response wasn't great for everybody, because they were all pissed off. Sometimes that happens."

Saturday, the 29th would feature the most acts during a single day, as twelve wildly musically varied performers took the stage. But perhaps it was *too* varied – most of the attendees were ready to rock along to the likes of Hendrix, the Who, and the Doors. When folk singer/guitarist Joni Mitchell hit the stage early, trouble soon started. A clearly "out of it" gentleman hopped up on stage uninvited, which led to the crowd voicing its disapproval when he was forcibly removed from the stage.

Lerner: "There was a famous scene where the crowd was yelling and yelling, and keeping her from singing. One guy came on the stage to try and interrupt her. She decided to face down the crowd, and was playing the piano, vamping, and almost crying. Said to the crowd, 'We've put our lives into this stuff – you're acting like tourists.' That changed the whole tenor of it. That was a very dramatic scene. Some people were afraid – she decided not to be afraid, she told me. She called the crowd 'The Beast' and she decided to face them down. Because she had had problems with other places, and had given in. But she decided in this case not to give in."

"I would say it was always on tenterhooks – was the crowd going to rush the stage? If they did, that would be the end. I was always worried about that, but they never did. It was really frightening when she was on. It's hard to imagine when you have those many people in front of you, I can tell you that. I was always worried, because I didn't understand what 'a crowd' was until that festival. Then I realized there was nothing you can do – if the crowd moves, than it's the end. You saw it in the Cincinnati thing [when fans were crushed to death trying to enter a Who concert in 1979]."

Although Lerner pointed out that Mitchell had earned the crowd's respect by the end of her set, the crowd's reaction prevented what would have undoubtedly been a festival highlight. According to the 1995 book *The Visual Documentary* by John

Robertson, Neil Young was going to duet with Mitchell, but changed his mind after witnessing the friction – leaving the festival before the end of Mitchell's set.

Since the crowd was on edge, it didn't seem like the wisest idea to put Tiny Tim on next – a gentleman best known in the US for his TV talk show appearances, and for strumming the ukulele/singing in an impenetrable falsetto. But Lerner was in for a big surprise. "Tiny Tim the audience went wild for! Because it was like a campy reaction. You would have thought that he was the biggest star in the world." Although his band didn't play until the following evening, Jethro Tull's Ian Anderson also remembers Tiny Tim at the Isle of Wight – but for other reasons. "I will always remember Tiny Tim, who seemed an innocuous fellow, in a rather James Brown/Chuck Berry kind of vein, refusing to go onstage until he had the money in cash in a briefcase, at his feet. Not exactly in that with the spirit of the age."

With Tiny Tim's set completed and the crowd "back on track," Miles Davis stepped up to the mic. In the midst of his groundbreaking jazz-fusion period (which would see the release of two all-time classics, 1969's *Bitches Brew* and 1970's *A Tribute to Jack Johnson*), the famous trumpeter/band leader had the crowd in the palm of his hand, remembers Lerner.

"Miles Davis was a surprise and really unusual. A really great performance. I liked his electric period, so I thought this was great. It was a revelation. It had pieces of *Bitches Brew* in it and stuff like that, but it was an amalgamation of different things. I was amazed that he was there, and the crowd really liked it. It was fantastic – he just went on and played, waved his hand at that audience, and walked off. And that was it. [Laughs] He played for approximately 38 minutes straight, without stopping. I wondered whether it was going to be accepted by the audience, or whether I would like it."

After Ten Years After had laid some more blues rock on the enormous throng, the second-ever performance by prog rockers Emerson Lake and Palmer unfolded. ELP's singer/ bassist, Greg Lake, recalls the vastness of the crowd. "The enduring memory is the actual physical sight of that many people. It was the first time in my entire life I'd seen that many people all together at one time. I supposed before that time, the only other time you'd see that many people gathered together, would have been a war. It was the first time in peace time that that many people had assembled in one place – peacefully – to listen to music. At least that I had seen. So it was a staggering sight to look at. It was also the second show of ELP. So that was kind of bizarre. The night before we had played to something like a thousand people, and then the next day, it was 600,000. So it was a shock."

Lake also remembers the festival not exactly reflecting the "peace and love" vibe of the times. "The whole nature of those festivals – Woodstock and the Isle of Wight – there was a kind of random chaos taking place. In a way, it was all meant to be relaxed and 'peace, love, and have a nice day,' but there kind of was a tension about the whole thing. Because of the vastness of it, there was this tension going on all the time. And of course, you had some very important entertainers on the bill. It was a highly charged event – sort of cosseted in this 'hippie/anything goes' cloak. It was a strange sort of dichotomy of elements, really. And that was more or less my memory. The actual playing of the show was over very fast, and one concert tends to feel much like another one. You do the best you can, and most of it is out of your control – other than the playing, really."

The crowd's response to ELP was very receptive, according to Lake. "It was a shock to the system, and we were very different from all the other acts on the bill. I think mainly because the music that we were playing was largely European-influenced, as opposed to most of the other music on the festival, was really, in one way or another, American-influenced. So there was a difference in that point of view."

Lake and company also managed to dodge a possibly disastrous situation, when a stage prop went awry. "The one thing we did decide to do for a bit of a spectacle, we decided to fire these 19th century cannons, at the end of 'Pictures at an Exhibition' – to sort of emulate 'The 1812 Overture.' It was just a bit of a stunt really, and what happened was unbeknownst to us in the band, the road crew had doubled the charge in the cannons. We had tested them the day before for safety, with the appropriate charge in. But they had somehow decided overnight that it would be cleverer to double it."

"So when it came time to fire these things, we had it on a footswitch. Keith [Emerson, keyboards] and I both pressed the footswitch at the same time, and all I can remember was seeing this solid iron huge cannon leave the ground! It just took off. It blew a couple of people off the stage, and it was of course a silly thing to do, because it could have been potentially extremely dangerous. But luckily enough, there was obviously no cannonball in it, thank God! So the charge just blew out, but it was so powerful that it lifted the thing off the stage. That was the one shock of the performance."

Similar to Santana's performance at Woodstock, it was ELP's show-stealing performance at the Isle of Wight that catapulted their career. Lake: "After that festival, the very next day, ELP was the front page of every newspaper. It was indeed one of those 'star overnight' situations."

One of the more intriguing performances would be up next – the Doors. Then in the midst of singer Jim Morrison's trial in Miami, Florida (for supposedly exposing himself during a performance), the band was granted permission to briefly leave the US to perform at the Isle of Wight. According to Lerner, the Doors weren't going to change their approach for anybody. "The thing about it that was interesting to me was Jim Morrison, who I knew, said, 'I don't think you're going to get an image because our lights are so low – but we're not going to change it.' I said, 'I'll get an image.' Which I did, I got some beautiful images by looking into the light, and making it surrealistic and abstract. It was just hypnotic, because of that way of doing it. I liked it a lot – the performance – it was low key. [Morrison] said, 'We want the world and we want it now!' I forgot what song that's from ['When the Music's Over'], but he was screaming during that."

"They had to leave right after the

performance – they were on trial in Miami. They were let out just for that performance, because of money, so they had to leave right away. They were in a low-key mood. But I was really hypnotized by the way I photographed it and the way by looking into the light, going in and out of focus. I know that a fan magazine of the Doors said it was a fantastic performance. The crowd was quiet – big and they seemed to like it. There was no yelling during it, that I could hear. Plus, they were very tired, the audience."

If the crowd was momentarily hypnotized by the Doors, they were about to be walloped back to their senses by the Who. Then still plugging their classic *Tommy* set, the Who handed in a stellar performance – considered one of the finest of their entire career.

Lerner: "They consider that one of their best performances. The Who performance was really fantastic – a great, theatrical presentation – with huge spotlights behind them that dazzled you. But also, 'Young Man Blues' and the new song, 'Water,' I thought was really fantastic. The ending of *Tommy* was really incredible. And 'Naked Eye' was great – 'Naked Eye' they had the lights on behind them also. 'Water' also was a new song at the time, and they said it was about Woodstock."

"In my interview with Pete [from the 2004 Who DVD, *Live at the Isle of Wight Festival 1970*], I got into the philosophical aspect of a song like 'Water.' It's kind of interesting, because 'Water' has a lot to do with – I'm being highfalutin – salvation and the philosophy of his guru [Meher Baba]. I said, 'Was 'Water' spiritual?' And he said, 'Yes.' But I said, 'The rest of the song is 'And somebody's daughter'.' So he said, 'I wrote that for Roger!' [Laughs] So there's that aspect of his relationship with Roger."

"And of course, Keith Moon was fantastic – playing around and having fun. He was in good shape while he was playing. I don't know what happened afterwards. [Laughs] As Pete says in this interview, often [Moon] was revved up, and then when he got off the stage, he would collapse or throw up. But he took a lot of stuff to get himself in 'good shape' – energetic shape, let's put it that way." [Laughs]

If the promoters were attempting to follow through with the claims of the 1970 Isle of Wight Festival being the UK version of Woodstock, it was on this evening that it became quite apparent, as three 'Woodstock veterans' closed the evening – the Who, folk/pop songstress Melanie, and multi-member funkateers, Sly and the Family Stone.

Sly and company were one of the world's top acts by this point – mixing social commentary with songs that appealed to both rock and dance fans. Family Stone sax player, Jerry Martini, recalls a not-so-smooth arrival. "I remember we had to fly in on a little two engine private jet. It was really windy and shaky – especially going back from there. Some girl was screaming at the top of her lungs. Because they didn't just have the band members, they had other people [too] – they were just shuttling us back and forth."

"I remember the beautiful cobblestone streets, and we stayed at a hotel that had a night club there. It was just really neat. I remember the concert was really happening. However, we did White City

Stadium in London at the same time – the Isle of Wight was on a series of concerts that we did. We did White City Stadium in London [and] Frankfurt, Germany – the Ferman Island [Festival] was the last one. It was exciting for us. We did well."

Martini also remembers that the crowd was receptive. "It was good. I don't remember any bad things at all. I just remember us playing our concert, going over well, and having a great time at the night club that they had there. Jam packed – it was probably the only nightclub they had at the time. I remember leaving that with a good feeling."

While Sly and the Family Stone's performance at the Isle of Wight went off without a hitch, Martini admits that it wasn't quite as magical a performance as a certain previous performance. "I don't think it was as good as Woodstock for us. Woodstock did the most for us, but it was way up there." And while other acts experienced problems at the Isle of Wight, Martini says it was nothing compared to another show the band was about to play.

"We did well at every concert, except Fehmarn Island on the Baltic Sea, which we didn't even play, because it was total chaos there. It was raining and storming, and there was a German gang there, they were shooting guns off – it was a nightmare. Jimi played though, but they were going nuts. It was rumored that the promoter got shot, because there was a German gang shooting off automatic weapons. I remember crawling on my hands and knees on the mobile they had there for us – glass was breaking everywhere. It was kind of scary."

Sunday, the 30th would be the final full day of performances – featuring the gentleman who many considered to be the headliner of the whole 1970 Isle of Wight Festival, Mr. Jimi Hendrix. In the morning, an ill-advised attempt was made to clear out the enormous audience for Jethro Tull's soundcheck, to ensure that those without a 'five day pass' would pay the fee for the day's festivities. According to Lerner, the scene soon turned ugly.

"[Tull's] soundcheck was very dramatic in the sense that they tried to empty the arena during the soundcheck – a famous scene. Of course, they couldn't. People had one day tickets as well as overall tickets, so they figured, people would just stay and not pay. The attempt to empty the arena was really funny – it was impossible. Then they said, 'They're not going to do a soundcheck unless you leave, then [Tull's] manager Terry Ellis said, 'Don't tell them that, because we don't care if they're here.' Kind of a nice scene – very dramatic."

"They tried all sorts of things to try to get rid of the people but they couldn't. They were all very tired – they'd been up all night. They were saying stupid things, and they thought the radicals were French, who were giving them a hassle. So the announcer that worked for the festival said, 'Hey, does anyone here speak French?' So out of nowhere, this girl came. And of course, spoke French very crudely, so the whole crowd was snickering. Then she really got into being part of the administration, and said, 'If you haven't paid, you've got to leave.' She said, 'I'll know what we'll do – those people who have tickets, burn your tickets, and then we'll know you have a ticket.' She said, 'Let's see these fires.' It was stupid. You're talking about 100,000 people, they weren't going to leave easily." Soon, the audience was throwing debris at the stage.

Around this time, a van of young hopefuls pulled up to the site of the festival – in hopes of being granted permission to play an impromptu set. It was agreed that they could indeed – but *outside* the festival. That band was space rockers Hawkwind. Hawkwind leader Dave Brock still remembers the day well. "We all decided we would head off to the Isle of Wight, it's one of those sort of 'iconic' sort of festivals, and go and play there outside. Which is what we did! The festival itself was quite a nice spot actually. What you've got to remember is the Isle of Wight has some lovely chalk cliffs. But the actual festival itself had all of these big corrugated sheets – it was like a prison camp. Once you're inside the festival, you're in this corrugated prison camp."

"We of course didn't want to go in there, we just thought, 'OK, we'll set up our gear and play outside.' Outside the festival there was this big sort of 'Canvas City,' which was a gigantic sort of inflatable tent, which was blown up – it has a generator running it, blows the air up, and the whole thing gradually inflates up. Someone came along and said, 'Hey, would you like to play inside?' And we said, 'Yeah, we'd love to.' So we actually played inside this inflatable sort of tent. The generator ran out, and [the tent] started sinking down!"

Brock also recalls drugs being passed freely amongst the crowd. "We all took loads of LSD, of course. Our lead guitarist, Huey [Huw Lloyd Langton], freaked out very badly, because he'd been spiked up on some orange juice, that was in the front of our yellow van. Unfortunately, I had some as well. The worst thing was, when I went back to the van, someone said, 'Don't go in the van, because I think Huey is having a bad time.' I said, 'Why is that?' And he said, 'Oh, he drank somebody's orange juice – it was on the dashboard, it's spiked with LSD.' I went, 'Oh no!' And suddenly, I had this great rush come over me – I was all tingly and peculiar. It was very strange LSD, actually. I had this lady with me, who took me away up to the cliff tops for a walk, to try and calm me down."

Additionally, Brock recalls bedlam going on outside the gates of the festival, and also a close brush with one of rock's all-time great guitarists. "There were a lot of anarchists-going's ons. They were all into saying that when the festival has made enough money, then the fences should be down, and all the people outside should be allowed in. And of course, they started ripping the fences down. There was a lot of bad scenes – people threatening each other and all that. There were I suppose about 10,000 people outside the festival."

"When I was telling you about this 'Canvas City' deflating, Jimi Hendrix actually came in there, funny enough, to see what was going on. Because he sort of kept tabs on what was going on, and we had our saxophonist who had his face half painted silver. I think in the Hendrix set, he actually dedicated one of the numbers to 'the guy down in the front with a silver face,' which is Nik [Turner], our saxophonist at the time. Nik eventually got around to talking to him and asked him if he'd have a jam with us in this big canvas structure. But by the time he got there, it was deflating and people were all standing with their hands up trying to support the thing – it was about eight foot high."

Back inside the festival, an early standout performance of the day was the Paul Rodgers/Paul Kossoff-led Free – who was supporting their classic *Fire and Water* release, and monster hit "All Right Now." Lerner: "To me, they were a revelation. I had never heard them before. I thought they were fantastic – their energy and their sensibility. And 'All Right Now' to me was really a thrilling song – it was very unusual, I didn't know what it was a blend of. It wasn't hard rock, yet it was rock."

Soon after Free's set, another performer impressed Lerner – the Moody Blues. "I think it was at twilight, and the lighting was unusual. I liked the singing, which was a little different – it was more melodic than most of the other groups. Especially 'Nights in White Satin.' I guess they were progressive rock, but speaking as a person who didn't know that much about it at the time of the festival, Emerson Lake and Palmer was progressive rock – very different than the Moody Blues. I liked the sensibility they revealed when they sided with the crowd, essentially. They were sympathetic to the crowd – that I remember quite well, and the beauty of the light at the time they performed."

Hawkwind's Brock recalls making it into the main area, in hopes of catching the Moody Blues' set. "I saw the Moody Blues there, actually. Everything ran late there. After the fences came down, we actually went inside there to see some of the bands. I had that really strong acid during the day, and by that time, I'd been given a Mandrax – a sleeping tablet to calm me down. I think I feel asleep, which was a bit of a shame, because I was quite looking forward to seeing them!"

Hendrix's performance was now growing near and anticipation was building – there was only one more performer to go, Jethro Tull. Tull leader Ian Anderson has not-so-fond memories of the Isle of Wight, despite handing in a very strong performance. "Things were going around both backstage and front of house, in the sort of 'unpleasant department,' that made it a little unpleasant for everybody. But it was out of control, and the organizers were struggling to keep the thing from degenerating into something quite horrible."

"There were some unpleasant degrees of rioting, violence, and bad behavior – more than one group of people who were intent on wrecking the festival. It was perhaps a testimony to the local police and generally the welcoming residents of the Isle of Wight, that the thing happened at all. It could have gotten really nasty. And for a while, around the time that we were taking the stage – it was looking a little tense around that period of time." The tenseness soon subsided however, and Tull handed in one of the festival's best sets.

Interestingly, it was Tull's refusal to play Woodstock, that set up their Isle of Wight appearance. "We were invited to play Woodstock and we didn't, mainly because I didn't want to spend my weekend among a bunch of unwashed hippies. And I didn't really think it was a good thing for us to do from a career point of view. I think that may well have been proven right, because it was both the big moment and the last moment of our peers Ten Years After, who had been born of the same music stable –

in early Chrysalis Records and management side of things. Well, some other acts on there that did go on and survive pretty well, namely Joe Cocker and the Who. It was also too much of a defining moment for a brand new band. It would have been the beginning and the end for us, as it was for Ten Years After. So I think we were best off not doing that one. And the Isle of Wight Festival seemed like a bit of tamed fun, compared to Woodstock. As it turned out, I think it was a defining moment in that change from the hippie ideals to the rather dark and more pragmatic side of music."

It also turns out that Tull went on, knowing that getting paid for their services was going to be a chore. "Not only from the point of view of the audience, who were learning a few lessons, but also as was evident backstage amongst the behavior of some of the bands and musicians. We on the other hand knew we were unlikely to get paid, and determined fairly early on that this was something that we really just had to go through and try and keep a modicum of a smile on our faces. And get through with as least drama as possible. So we just kind of got on with it and did our bit. It was not a good gig, it was not a bad gig – it was just a little frenetic and a little tense."

With Tull's set completed and Hendrix's gear set and ready to go, the MC made a most-welcomed announcement. "Let's have a welcome for Billy Cox on bass, Mitch Mitchell on drums, and the man with the guitar, Jimi Hendrix." Finally, the performer that many of the 600,000 had come to see was about to launch into a near two hour-long set, which included old favorites, as well as previews from his next proposed album, *First Rays of the New Rising Sun*. But as evidenced by Hendrix's performance on the 2002 DVD, *Blue Wild Angel: Jimi Hendrix Live at the Isle of Wight*, something was wrong with one of the greatest guitarists of all-time. Hendrix appeared dazed throughout, while almost every song included a meandering guitar improv and a flubbed vocal line. Additionally, Hendrix appeared more concerned with constantly consulting with roadies then concentrating on the performance at hand.

As Pete Townshend reminisced in the 2001 DVD, *30 Years of Maximum R&B Live* – "What made me work so hard was seeing the condition that Jimi Hendrix was in. He was in such tragically bad condition physically. And I remember thanking God as I walked on the stage that I was healthy." Sly and the Family Stone's Jerry Martini agrees with Townshend's assessment. "His pants were falling down, [while] he was standing on stage. And I felt bad for him, because everybody in Sly and the Family Stone, including Sly, were really big fans of Jimi's. Everybody was concerned about Jimi's health. But at the time, everybody was afraid to talk to Sly or to Jimi about any problems, y'know? Usually, they have management and their representatives do that."

Murray Lerner admits that Townshend may have known more about what was going on behind the scenes than the director, since he was out front, filming the proceedings. "[Townshend] knew Hendrix better than I did. Yeah, he looked tired, but he really played well, I thought. You'd have to judge for yourself. I didn't think he was in bad shape, I just thought he was tired. He did great renditions of 'Red

House' and 'Machine Gun,' which I think is as good as anything he's ever done. I mean, there's a lot of different discussions about that concert and Hendrix. He didn't give the usual wild, waving around [performance], which I like. I think it wasn't just tiredness, but I think that he was starting to feel that he was through with all that other stuff – of putting on a show – and was more into playing his music. And other people have said that also, that he was looking forward to being that way, and starting to emphasize the music more than the theatrics."

Still, Lerner enjoyed Hendrix's performance, nonetheless. "He was pretty funny sometimes. He really just improvised, and before he went on, he said, 'How does 'God Save the Queen' go?' And then he played 'God Save the Queen.' He said, 'Everyone stand up for your country and your beliefs,' and as an aside, he said, 'And if you don't, fuck you.' Then of course, 'Machine Gun' is always great, but in this case, it was like, 'Here's a song for the skinheads in Birmingham,' and for this and that. And then he says, 'Oh yeah, and Vietnam, I almost forgot about that,' which of course, is not true – it's ironic. 'Machine Gun' was great, it goes on for about 17 minutes." Sadly, this would prove to be one of Jimi Hendrix's last ever performances. He would die just over two weeks later, at the age of 27.

Although many assume that Hendrix closed the 1970 Isle of Wight Festival, as he did a year earlier at Woodstock, this is a false assumption – Joan Baez and Leonard Cohen played in the wee hours, and Richie Havens closed the whole thing at daybreak.

Lerner recalls the last two performers of the

festival. "I remember [Cohen's set] was late at night. He said some very nice things about the radical movement of the time, saying, 'We're a small nation, but we're going to grow. We need our own land, we don't have it yet.' I remember he had a lot of beautiful women singing with him – I was jealous. He had that kind of attraction I think – the suffering poet." [Laughs]

"I don't consider [Havens] the last, because he played at dawn. For me, the last was Leonard Cohen. I think [Havens] wasn't on the stage – he was walking around singing off the stage. Singing at sunrise. It was very moving." With the end of Havens' set, the remainder of the dwindling crowd made its way for the exit – undoubtedly bleary eyed, hungry, and unwashed. Although catastrophe seemed to hover over the festival throughout its duration, it never came to a head.

There would obviously be other UK festivals in the wake of the turbulent 1970 Isle of Wight Festival, but it was now clear that all future gatherings could not get by merely on the "peace and love" ethos of the '60s. Rock festivals now spelt big business – with adequate facilities for the audience, proper security, and contracts that ensured that the artists receive their full monetary sums for performing.

Ian Anderson for one, was glad to see the "change of the guard," so to speak. "I have to say, I was never one for the kind of 'hippie thing,' and the rather laidback, and the UK rather louche, sort of druggie, arty behavior. I think it was a little different to how it was in the USA. But nonetheless, the sort of hippie thing as epitomized by some of those

British pop and rock bands – like Mick Jagger for example, was I suppose someone who readily slipped into that hippie, druggie, laidback thing. It was something that I always found quite distasteful. I didn't grow up with that kind of approach to life, and I didn't readily sort of linger within that kind of social embrace. It was interesting – at the Isle of Wight, that really started to crumble."

Bonus Bit #1: Jimi Hendrix, A Legend And A Friend
Sly and the Family Stone's Jerry Martini and Chicago's Walter Parazaider remember Hendrix.
Although Jimi Hendrix has gained a mythic stature since his death, two of the performers at the 1970 Isle of Wight Festival remember him as a mere mortal, and a good friend.

Jerry Martini: "Jimi was really good friends with the members of our band – a really nice guy. He didn't have that 'star attitude' like, 'Screw you, I'm better than you.' He was just a real gentleman. I saw him [shortly] before he died at the hotel at the Isle of Wight. It was a shame – well, everybody was getting high back then, but Jimi, he just over-did it."

Walter Parazaider: "Hendrix had taken us out on the road. We were playing the Whisky A-Go-Go in Hollywood – we got done playing, I was putting my saxes away, and all of a sudden, a guy tapped me on the shoulder, and it was Hendrix! In a very calm manner, he said, 'You three horn players are like one set of lungs, and your guitar player [the late Terry Kath] is better than me. I'd like to take you out on the road as my opening act'."

"I don't think I had ever met as kind a human

being – somebody who really wasn't ego'd out or full of himself that he didn't give a shit about other people. He was just a good human being, and he saw something in us that we didn't even see. He was generous enough to give us a shot at doing something. I said, 'How could we ever repay you for this, for how good you've been to us?' And he said, 'Pass it on.' Jimi was very articulate, but a very soulful guy. Yes, he was spiritual, and that guitar, he could make it talk."

"We'd sit on a plane and talk about different things. I'd say, 'Sometimes you seem real bummed out. How come you are?' And he said, 'You're going to know about this even more than me. You're going to have a lot of hit records, and you're going to have to play them night after night for people. I have hit records, and I have to play them night after night.' And I said, 'Is that such a bad thing?' And he said, 'You'll see how it'll be down the road.' I said, 'What would you rather do?' He said, 'I'd rather take my guitar and I'd rather take my old lady, and play every Southside bar anywhere in the world'."

Both musicians also recall an invitation from Hendrix to join him in the studio, signaling that he was eager to work horns into his sound. Parazaider: "He said, 'I'd like to take the horns in the studio and do an album with you'." Martini: "Every time I saw him, he'd ask me, 'Come on down to the studio man, come on down to the studio.' Which I never really went, because Sly didn't want us to record with anybody else but our band at the time. He wanted us to have more of a mystique. And I know that Jimi was really interested in getting [bassist] Larry Graham in the studio. It didn't really happen, but they had talked about it – because of Larry's innovative bass styling."

Bonus Bit #2: The Isle of Wight on DVD
Wondering where to find the aforementioned performances on DVD? Wonder no more...
With nearly all of the performers filmed by Murray Lerner, a few of the acts have issued their own DVD's, while others can be found as part of a compilation. To view what many consider to be the best performance of the entire festival, check out the Who's 2004 release, *Live at the Isle of Wight Festival 1970*. Long considered the greatest live rock band of all-time, this release confirms it once and for all, as the cameras capture arguably the group's best gig ever. The only complaint is that several key *Tommy* tracks are omitted, including "Amazing Journey/ Sparks."

Jethro Tull's 2005 release, *Nothing Is Easy: Live at the Isle of Wight 1970*, is also highly recommended, as the group hands in (according to Lerner), "a kinky, quirky performance." Heavy on the early obscurities however, and light on the renowned classics. The 2002 Jimi Hendrix release, *Blue Wild Angel*, is a true-to-form live document of the guitarist's set, warts and all, while the 2004 Miles Davis release, *Miles Electric: A Different Kind of Blue*, features some great jazz-fusion playing.

Lerner also finally released his "Isle of Wight movie" in 1997 ("I was a bad salesman," he jokes), *Message to Love: The Isle of Wight Festival*, which collects performance highlights and behind-the-scenes footage. According to Lerner, more Wight-related DVD releases are forthcoming – an ELP release is set for early 2006, and an agreement was met to release Joni Mitchell's set towards the end of 2006.

Additionally, Lerner is currently in discussions to release a DVD of the Doors' performance. Unfortunately, we will never see Chicago or Sly and the Family Stone's performances on DVD – both acts declined to be filmed.

*Reactions to the news of Jimi's tragic passing,
on September 18, 1970.*

FRANK MARINO: I remember I was going to the center of town where all the hippies hung out – we were hippies in those days – and I remember someone said, "Hey, look at this," and it was in the newspaper. I was pretty stunned. You know that kind of shocking "Come on...*that can't be true.*" And it was a short article – it was maybe a paragraph long, on like, page four of the newspaper. And it said something like, "MUSICIAN JIMI HENDRIX DIES AT 27." And you go looking through the paragraph to find out as much as you can about it [the cause of death on the death certificate lists "Inhalation of vomit, Barbiturate intoxication (quinalbarbitone), Insufficient evidence of circumstances open verdict"].

But people have to understand I was there at the time of Jimi Hendrix's rise and demise, and he was really not as appreciated towards the end of his three-year period as he was at the beginning. I believe that when he did Isle of Wight – which was one of the last gigs he did – he left the stage to a very small smattering of applause. He was really at a frustrated point, I think. Eric Burdon tells a story about Jimi having called him up to say, "Y'know what? I'm changing everything. I'm going to get a new band, I'm going to change my life – I'm fed up." And then that weekend, he died.

I think Jimi Hendrix in a sense was a very

tragic figure. *Extremely* tragic figure. And I think he had a lot of people around him that didn't really care as much for him than they cared for the brouhaha that they could make by him being there. I don't think they were really thinking of his best interests – let's put it this way.

RANDY HANSEN: I used to get a ride to school from my next-door neighbor – who was kind of a jerk. He was older than me. But I got a ride from him, anyway. He used to mess with me all the time. I got in his car that morning, and he goes, "Hey man, your man died." I go, "What?" *"Jimi Hendrix is dead."* I said, "You're a fucking liar." He goes, "No man, he's dead." "He's not dead! You're just fucking with me again!" I got really pissed at him – I got into a big argument with him on the way to school. And then I got to school, and that's all anybody was talking about. I was devastated. It was like my father dying all over again. That hurt.

BILLY SHEEHAN: I was in high school at the time. I remember seeing a kid at school with a black armband, and going, "What's going on?" "Didn't you hear?" "What?" "Jimi." "Jimi who?" "Jimi Hendrix died." *Unreal.* I was dazed over by it initially, then I found out the details later. I was just crushed – because we'll never have that again. We have the recordings…but we'll never have *that.*

The same when John Lennon died – we'll never have the Beatles again, as they are. And everyone from my generation – those songs, bands, the vibe, and the style, it was alive and it was *everything* to us. That's what we wore and what we spoke and how we walked and talked. So, when we lost someone like Jimi or John Lennon…it just tears a hole through you.

ULI JON ROTH: It was a complete shock, because I had just seen the man twelve days earlier – I was at his very last concert, at the Isle of Fehmarn, an island in Germany, in the Baltic Sea. And thanks to my father – who was a journalist – I had a backstage pass. So, I was very close to Hendrix there – before and after the show. But I didn't get to say anything, because I was just a 15-year-old kid, and he was obviously in a totally different world and mindframe that day.

And then suddenly…I was at school. Matthias Jabs was there, because he was one of the students at that school, and the reason was because I had a Vox AC30 amplifier, and they had a school party, and they asked me to borrow my amplifier as a PA system. I said yes, which is why I was there that day. Somebody suddenly mentioned that Hendrix had just died, and that was a great shock, because he was supposed to play in Hanover – our hometown – a couple of days later. I remember that. But all that got cancelled. It was a huge shock.

I remember going to some dark room – being totally depressed. And then somebody said, "Well, why don't you get up on stage and play?" And that's what I did. I played Jimi songs for about half an hour – on my AC30, with my guitar. That was that day.

KK DOWNING: That was a real shock. By then, I was aspiring to being a guitar player, myself. And Hendrix was my leading light. Everything from a newspaper or a magazine, I'd cut out the pictures and hang them on the bedroom wall – it was just *plastered.*

I was trying to hold down a job to get paid, to get a decent guitar and an amplifier. I came in from work one night, and my mother said, "Jimi Hendrix has died." I was in disbelief – *"How could this possibly happen?"* It was a big thing to a lot of people, but you can imagine I was the one person that I don't think could be more inspired by this one person – who this person was and what he did and what he achieved in such a short space of time. It was a massive blow, as it was to the world.

RIK EMMETT: It was a tragedy. It was sadness. I was still in high school, and when you're young, there's a million other things going on in your life, and that seems like something that is removed – a long way away from whatever my life was at the time. But that whole thing of how, now, this is Rik Emmett a 66-year-old, pretty straight forward kind of guy, looking at life now. But I was probably a little bit angry – seeing it as, "Why would you indulge so heavily in drugs that you're going to choke to death on your own vomit?" kind of thing. It happens in the rock culture, and I never liked it. I always thought it was a tragic waste.

So, there was probably a part of me – even when I was a teenager – where I was like, "Well, the only person to blame is him." You hate to do it, because a lot of people around are seeing him as an object of pity, and their sadness is profound, because they don't see the person is at fault for their own problem, y'know? But I tend to be maybe a little more pragmatic than that. I think, "Well...you didn't necessarily *have to* do that much drugs. And you didn't *need to* combine medications at the same time – that's probably been a part of it." So, it's choices. I don't know...now I'm being a moralist and being on a high horse, and I don't like doing it. But nevertheless, I probably at the time thought, "Well, that's too bad. But you've got yourself to blame for that." Again, a lack of discipline.

And of course, the cult springs up – there are books you can get now, about "the 27 Club." Cobain is part of it now, too. It's part of the culture. And here *you* are – you're interviewing people because you're going to write a book about Hendrix. Well, it's quite possible – it's plausible – to me, that if he hadn't died a tragic young death, then he might have become a little more human over time. But because that never happens, now, he's become iconic. It's like, Christ dying on the cross at 33. You get this icon that had this early, tragic thing, and so the cult is now going to form.

And again, I hate to sound too pragmatic, but an industry will spring up around somebody who dies young, because, "Oh...we can really milk this. We don't have to pay the guy – all we're paying is his estate. So, we can put ourselves in the position where we can become the middle man, and we can profit from the fact that this guy died young." So, record companies, publishing companies...it springs up. It happens in jazz, it happens in rock. In fact, there's a movie out now about Judy Garland! [Laughs] So, there is a fascination that we're going to have with people that die young, that had such gifts.

MICK BOX: It was a shock. But a lot of things were happening around that time. The whole industry in those early days, the drug things were not just in with the artists – it went right through the industry. So, *everyone* was doing it. And it was all a good laugh and a bit fun...until people started to pass away. And then you got the Jimi Hendrixes, the Janis Joplins, the Jim Morrisons dying, and you thought, "This isn't as much fun as we think it is." And that's when people started to take a second look at it and take a step back. Simply because of how much he achieved while he was on the earth, you wonder where the hell he would have ever gone with it. You can't even conceive of where it would have gone.

MICHAEL SCHENKER: I had heard when Jimi had died – without actually knowing much of his music, because I was only 15 years old. I was playing a pinball machine, and somebody came in, and said, "Jimi Hendrix died!"

SCOTT GORHAM: It's one of those days where you go, "Anybody but *him*." I remember thinking the same thing when Stevie Ray Vaughan died. We all know everybody's not going to live forever and they're going to die, and it kind of bounces off you – "What a drag." But then, there are "those guys," that when they go, it kind of affects you. And definitely, Hendrix and Stevie Ray were the two guys that did it to me.

ALEX LIFESON: Of course his death was a shock. But I do recall thinking he didn't look very healthy leading up to it.

ADRIAN BELEW: I couldn't believe his life was being cut short that quickly. He only had three years to show us his world! It was a reckless era where the drug culture had already veered tragically wrong and many of our most talented artists – who were living stressful realities – were unable to cope. A very, very sad thing.

PAUL LEARY: I actually remember that day. I was sitting at the dining room table with my family, and we had a new Sylvania TV set that was sort of adjacent to the dining room, and I had a seat at the dining room table that I could turn, look, and see the TV. The news was on – probably Walter Cronkite or something – and they announced the news of his passing. It was shocking. Things were different back then – in regards to drugs. I mean, people almost thought of drugs in a cool, hip, kinda funny way. Before the "dying off" started, I don't think anybody really understood the magnitude. Cocaine was considered cool – it was "a rich people's drug," and everybody wanted to be rich.

BRUCE KULICK: I was in my mother's kitchen in Queens…and what can I say? I was just devastated. I was *so* angry. There would have been so much more for him to create and do. But he was just one of many dying at that magical age of 27. Very weird.

DAVID GIVENS [Zephyr bassist]: When Hendrix died, Eddie Kramer [who was producing Zephyr's next album, *Going Back to Colorado*, at Electric Lady] called and said, "We won't be recording today – *Jimi's dead.*" Tommy Bolin's reaction to learning of Jimi's death was just a shocked look – I'm the one who told him. Eddie called me, and I went over to [Tommy's] room and told him what was up. He did a wide-eyed double take. We were all amazed. Eddie was going to introduce us – we were expecting to meet him, and then, suddenly, he was no more.

We went down to the studio – pretty corny, but we wanted to play some of Hendrix's songs as sort of a tribute, because he was our hero. He and Miles Davis were our heroes. So we went in there, and Jimi's black Stratocaster was there. We all walked over and went, "Whoa!" Tommy put his hand on the guitar. Then we played "Hey Joe" and "Foxy Lady." Then the electronics guy – Shimon I think was his name, an Israeli guy – was super pissed that we were in there. He started yelling at us – and I understand, Jimi was his friend, and on top of that, his world had come to an end. He kicked us out of the studio.

That record was a mess because after Hendrix died, the fight went out of Eddie Kramer completely. He was totally preoccupied with trying to get *Cry of Love* done – which I understand. The thing is, Jimi was deeply involved in the mixing and production. So for Mitch and Eddie to try and put that together without him...I mean, they were asking *us* for help! We picked a couple of songs that went on that album – me and Tommy – because they just didn't know what to do. One of them was "Belly Button Window," I can't remember what the other one might have been.*

*Quote is from the 2008 book, *Touched by Magic: The Tommy Bolin Story*, by Greg Prato.

STEVE VAI: No, I didn't know. I was ten when I discovered the *Woodstock* 8-track. That was right around when he passed, so I had no connection to the outside world in that way. I mean, there was no internet, it wasn't on TV really...or if it was, I missed it. Or maybe it happened beforehand. I think he probably passed before I listened to all that stuff.

I didn't know, so I thought, "Why would I think this guy is dead," y'know? So, I built up this incredible desire to see him play. And then somebody said, "No, you can't see Hendrix – *he's dead.*" It was just like a rude awakening. And then somebody said, "He died from a drug overdose." So there were all these kind of signals that you get from the outside. I remember feeling very let down when I discovered it.

KIRK HAMMETT: I think if Jimi would have survived, he would have heard Mahavishnu Orchestra, he would have heard all this progressive stuff, he would have heard all this fusion – like the Headhunters and whatnot – he would have heard what Jeff Beck was doing, he would have heard Jaco Pastorius. I think he would have went into a voodoo-jazz-fusion-funk kind of direction.

This is just me projecting...but I think he would have gone in that direction. And also, with the influence of people like Zappa, as well. And like I said, Mahavishnu...and Santana, too. I think Carlos would have been a huge influence on Jimi – in terms of all the percussion. That's the direction I think he would have gone into. I picture an older Jimi Hendrix with dreadlocks probably – at some point in the late

'70s. [Laughs] And shorter hair and glasses in the '80s.

CURT KIRKWOOD: It could have. [In response to the question "Did Jimi dying young add to his legend?"] It's hard to say. Maybe not going on made it so he didn't do anything goofy. Some people said he was on his way to inventing disco – I've heard that. But who knows?

REVEREND HORTON HEAT: It's a shame for him – he for sure did not live to really reap the benefits of the "Jimi Hendrix thing." It really makes you wonder what would have happened. Like everybody in the music business, he probably would have fell out of favor – "That guy had some hits back in the '60s. Jimi Hendrix…*whatever*." I'm not sure what would have happened to him. I'm sure he'd still be considered influential, obviously.

BILLY SHEEHAN: But on the other band, as controversial as it might be – and as much flak as I might get for saying so – when an artist dies, he stops at *that* point. And he never sucks – he never gets old, fat, falls apart, has bad shows, has a public divorce with his wife, gets arrested for domestic abuse, or whatever happens to people when they go on. So, it's horrible to lose him – and I wish he was back and lived for as long as nature would have allowed – but as an artist, to have such a stopping point, it is pretty amazing to have the body of work that he has. It will always shine as a result.

RANDY HANSEN: I've had a lot of wild experiences at Jimi's grave [at Greenwood Memorial Park in Renton, Washington]. Once, I played the Isle of Fehmarn – that was Jimi's last gig – and they gave me his room at the hotel, and a bunch of personal pictures that the hotel owners took of him. They put them all in a binder and gave them to me. That was the end of our tour, also.

I got home, and now, it was September 18th – the day that Jimi died. I was having a meeting with this Japanese lady – about possibly going to Japan. It turned out she wanted to try and join my band – she was lying about trying to bring us to Japan. I turned her down, and then she said, "I heard Jimi was buried here. Can you take me to his grave?" I said, "Sure." This is one of three weird things that happened to me. But this is probably the weirdest one.

I'm taking her out there…now, I have to go back a little bit in time, because they announced one time over the radio here in Seattle that I was dead. And it was because a guy named Randy Hansen in White Center [in Washington] died – and that's right where I lived, was in White Center. I didn't realize there was another "Randy Hansen" living there. So, he died, and the word went out over the radio that I was dead. And my mom and my sister heard it, freaked out, and called me – "Are you alright? They're announcing over the radio that you're dead. You need to call the radio station." So, I called them up and said, "*Stop announcing that I'm dead.*" Because I knew these guys. So, that was a weird thing that affected my career quite a bit – because after that, my manager called to try and get a new gig, and they'd say, "No. *Randy's dead.*" It was quite a few gigs that I didn't get again, because supposedly…I was dead!

Anyway, now I'm up at Jimi's grave with this Japanese lady. And there's two guys standing there. And it's a nice day out. So, I'm up there, walk up to them and say, "Hey, nice day." "Yeah, nice day." We started yapping back and forth. And they asked, "Did you know Jimi?" I said, "No. But I knew his dad." And his dad was buried right next to him at this point, and I pointed to his grave. They said, "You look like a musician." I said, "Yeah, I am." "What's your name? Maybe we heard of you." I say, "Randy Hansen." The guy goes, "That was my father's name. He died about a year-and-a-half ago." I said, "In White Center?" He goes, "How did you know that?" And I said, "Because it started a rumor that *I* was dead." And I'm going, "Wait a minute…I just came from Isle of Fehmarn, and now, I'm meeting Randy Hansen's son over Jimi Hendrix's grave on September the 18th!"

All the other stories are too long to tell you. One isn't – the first time I was ever there, I had a photographer friend of mine that used to take a lot of pictures of me. The first picture he takes of me at Jimi's grave, he had a developing room, and he develops it, and there's what looks like the outline of Jimi Hendrix in white – like a ghost – standing behind me in the picture. I was like, "You did this." He's like, "No, I swear to God! Look, here's the negative."

These are the kinds of things that make you believe in an afterlife.

Chapter 24
James Marshall Hendrix

Why Jimi's music has stood the test of time and
continues to inspire.

KK DOWNING: It's just so timeless, isn't it? Everything he did was very timeless. Put it this way, guitar players...*really, really good* guitar players – like Zakk Wylde, Stevie Ray Vaughan, Frank Marino – these guys play, and it sounds great. And obviously, they sound like Hendrix because they are influenced by Hendrix, but if these players try and do their own songs/versions of Hendrix, and play Hendrix's style, they sound just like Hendrix.

Hendrix, that whole style of guitar player, is attributable to Hendrix's musical ability and technique – to amalgamate major and minor pentatonic scales, and not be afraid to incorporate major chords into his playing. He had the whole thing, really. He was able to move from major to minor in a way that nobody really did. And his technique – certainly for the '60s, because he barely went into the '70s – it's quite phenomenal, really. It's *absolutely* phenomenal.

ADRIAN BELEW: When you listen to his records they're still so powerful, they have such authority and raw excitement. I don't care what age you are, when you hear Jimi Hendrix, you know something extraordinary is going on there. He was a great bluesman, a profound virtuoso, and a bold futurist – all in one person. His lyrics reflected a dreamy universe only *he* lived in. And his performances were riveting. Though many people have tried, I knew when I saw him perform, no one would ever be able to do that again.

MICK BOX: I think it's endured because it's *real*. It's like all the bands from the '70s, all the music has stood the test of time because it's real – people are going in and playing live, they're not sharing files across the world. There's none of that. You need to define a specific style and you make it up, or you experimented. You didn't just go to a keyboard and put one finger on a key. It was real, honest, and *played* – that comes through the grooves. And by doing that, you get good feel in everything. Amazing feel on everything. And that's what gets through to you, and gives you the chills in the spine, and the hairs on your arms stand up.

RIK EMMETT: It had its unique qualities – and *still* does. I mean, there are guys that are trying to imitate Hendrix. You can listen to it, and go, "Oh...they're trying to imitate Hendrix." It has its own unique qualities – that would be one of the first things I would say. It exists on an extremely high level – his technical proficiency on playing guitar, his sort of physical gift, is really high.

DOUG PINNICK: The thing about Hendrix is everybody knows Hendrix songs like everybody knows Beatles songs. We don't know where we heard it, we don't know how we heard it...but they're just in our heads. I think I probably know more Hendrix songs than any other band in the world.

KIM THAYIL: The baby boom is still alive, so the baby boom is embracing the nostalgia of their youth – so they'll rush out and buy a new Beatles record, a new Hendrix record if it's a good one, and they'll turn their kids on to it, and their kids may reference it, as well. I think as long as Hendrix is brought up as a reference in guitar magazines and from father to daughter or mother to son, I think that Hendrix will have his place, and there will be young guys that say, "Yeah! I learned this from 'Purple Haze'."

Hendrix turns up in a lot of movies about the '60s and the Vietnam War – and so do the Stones. If you ask me, I think there should be more Mothers of Invention, Velvet Underground, and MC5 music in Vietnam War movies – but music directors, what do they know? That's why they put in the Stones, Hendrix, and the Doors *every fucking time*. I think as long as popular culture refers nostalgically and romantically to the heyday and salad days of the baby boom, then things like Jimi Hendrix will be relevant and referred to – at least in terms of pop culture. And he'll constantly be referred to in terms of his place in the lineage of rock n' roll and rock guitar evolution.

It seems like the "era of the guitar gods" is kind of waning – it seems to be less important to the Millennial generation than it was to Baby Boomers and Gen Xers. I think Gen Xers cared less about those elements. But as long as he's referred to, people will go back and say, "Ah. *This* is how the different elements came to be together. *This* is how this works. *This* is how you incorporate all these different ways of being a musician." As long as he's referenced that way, then he will be relevant.

PAUL LEARY: Why does music stand the test of time? It was just passing it through a genius – it's a gift that very few people have.

BRIAN TATLER: Probably because it's brilliant! [Laughs] And most people can appreciate talent when they see it – *raw* talent. So, I would just think there is no denying Jimi Hendrix. It's no gimmick, is it? It's just incredibly brilliant what Hendrix laid down. Even though I never saw him, it's there on tape. Fortunately, people had the foresight to capture what he was doing – for future generations.

KIRK HAMMETT: It's really, really simple – because there's so much emotion, so much feeling, and so much soul. There is a wide, wide palette of feelings and emotions and soul. And the music is just *dripping* with it – all of his music is just dripping with so much soul and passion. I mean, you can take a current event right now – Black Lives Matter. OK, listen to "House Burning Down" – that song is about the Watts riots. And it's *totally* relevant now. It's amazing. Or, you take a song like "Belly Button Window" – it's about a child that is looking out their mother's bellybutton, and going, "Wow. Do I *really* want to come out and be a part of this reality? It might just be better me staying in here!" And how relevant is that right now?

    And his music still sounds fresh because it's still so difficult to reproduce. When people copy Jimi Hendrix's solos…*no one* can ever reproduce a Hendrix song like Jimi can. And thank God. Because when people cover it, it's almost a barometer for their own personality and own expression. You can't copy

Jimi Hendrix and expect it to sound like Jimi Hendrix. I feel that if you cover a song, you shouldn't set out for it to be just like the original...because we already have the original. I think it's a better idea when you're covering songs to make it as different as possible to the original. And so, because of the emotions that are in Jimi Hendrix's songs, when a person covers it, their *own thing* just comes out. It's like a gateway or an opening to their own sound. Jimi's songs are a platform for that.

EAST BAY RAY: Like I said, make the familiar sound different or the different sound familiar. He rocked really well, he had ear-catching melodies, ear-catching guitar licks, good lyrics – all the things that we consider talent. And a lot of it is you're either born with it or you're not. And if you're born with it, then you also have to get the technical skills that he communicated to other people. He had *all* that.

The thing is, he really didn't use a lot of clichés in his music. A lot of guitar players are great, but they're doing licks that are off of somebody else – old blues licks or old heavy metal licks. He didn't really do that...*sometimes*, but most of the time he didn't. His playing is very soulful. And he can play blues – that *Blues* record is pretty amazing. I like the blues, but his Jimi Hendrix Experience records are *not* blues records. [Laughs] They're rock records...acid rock, I guess.

CURT KIRKWOOD: He's one of a kind. That's what happens – it's like, you don't have somebody that paints like van Gogh, you don't have somebody else that plays like Jimi.

RANDY HANSEN: Absolutely [Jimi is the greatest rock guitarist of all-time]. Without a doubt. No one can touch him. I don't think anybody ever will with the guitar – not unless they can maybe, I don't know…set themselves on fire, play, and then live through it!

PAUL LEARY: You could argue a lot about second place. But yeah, absolutely. He's in the hall of fame. There was cool rock guitar before...but he let the beast loose.

KK DOWNING: I think he was the greatest, because he came along at a time when everything hadn't been done and everything hadn't been invented and presented. But he came with the whole package, really. Everybody else was left to pick up the pieces, to go and design something also unique, that hadn't been done. And it was really bloody hard work – it took us *years* to perfect it. But Hendrix, way back then in the '60s, he was there. Where the hell did that come from? It was a lightning bolt from another year or something…that landed on a stage somewhere.

DOUG PINNICK: There always will be somebody greater – whether we know it or not. I believe that he is in the hall of the greatest of the greatest – let's put it that way. And I would put him at #1 in *my* greatest book.

SCOTT GORHAM: I would say Stevie Ray Vaughan actually played better versions of Hendrix songs than Hendrix did. But I think what Hendrix did was he actually showed the world what you could do with a guitar. He was the one that broke the dam for everybody. I still listen today to things that Hendrix did, and go, "Fuck...that is *so* beautiful. That is unbelievable." But as far as being "the best ever," no, I don't think that. But Hendrix will always be a hero of mine – absolutely. I think he was the guy that said, "If you see Clapton doing that, well, now look at what *you* can do." And that's when everyone went, "Fuck man...the guitar is a lot more intricate than we all thought it could be."

BRIAN TATLER: My favorite is Jimmy Page. Because of his songwriting and his breadth, really – his ability to write, produce, solo, acoustic, different tunings. Led Zeppelin are my favorite band...so that's all I can say, really. I mean, Hendrix is in the top-5.

STEVE VAI: I would say based on the perspective of how people value what a great guitar player is, yes – Jimi Hendrix *was* probably the greatest guitar player of all-time. But that's a completely subjective statement, because he might not be to everybody. And if there is one person that doesn't agree, then he's not. But yeah, I have absolutely no trouble saying in my mind that Jimi Hendrix was the greatest guitar player of all-time. Because of the awareness that he brought to the instrument for all of us. The awareness of his capabilities in the genre that most of us loved – which is rock.

But given my choice of sitting down and listening to a guitar player, I'll go to Allan Holdsworth every time...not *every* time, you know what I mean – if I have a pull to listen to really stimulating guitar playing, for me, I listen to Allan Holdsworth. If I want to hear Hendrix, I like to listen to some of those newer recordings that have come out – those "secret recordings" that were outtakes in the studio. You hear so much in those – you can really hear his brilliance. His on-the-edge creativity in the moment without any excuses. But yeah, as far as what he brought to the world, and the way that the world measures these things, I think that's an accurate statement.

BILLY SHEEHAN: It's hard for people now…I see young guitarists listen to Hendrix now, and they're like, "Eh, it's OK I guess. He's a little out of tune and he's not playing very fast." By today's standards, yeah. But back then, when that came out – it blew *everybody's* mind. Nobody had ever heard that kind of feedback, distortion, and playing the way he did. As often, younger players forget about the timeline and try to insert it into today's timeline. Yeah, Yngwie technically is a monstrous player that few players can play as good as…or Steve Vai or any other number of players.

But if you put it in a timeframe and go back to where it was, we were just coming out of an era where guitar solos were not that much. I played at a time where it was more important to have a B3 in your band than it was to have a guitar player! You needed that more than a guitar player, because you didn't have those many guitar solos – it wasn't *that* important.

Then Hendrix came out, and it became "a guitar world." It's a complicated thing, but I think people often forget the actual timeline that happened there. When Jimi came out, we didn't have that. And then after he came out, we did. So, looking at it from today's point of view, it might seem kind of tame in some people's eyes – not mine, because I lived through it. But man, it changed *everything*.

KIRK HAMMETT: Yeah, I would say that [Jimi is the greatest rock guitarist of all-time]. Only because it's hard to put anybody else in that position. And it's easy to put Jimi in that position, because he died at 27. And look at all he accomplished in that short amount of time – like, five years, maybe. To accomplish all of that in that short period of time and be *so* influential, to leave a body of music that is still vibrant and influential to this day – to this minute – I would say yes, he is probably the greatest guitar player. To be able to do all that in that short of time…I mean, there are *lots* of great guitar players out there. But they had the benefit of their whole lives playing and getting better and exploring and shifting and changing. *Jimi didn't have that.* He came out and he was all he was in those five years.

RIK EMMETT: I think that you always want the best of somebody to be the thing that survives, and I think in Hendrix's case, it did. His records are still there for everyone, and certainly, his influence as a guitarist is never-ending. In the history of guitar playing, there are some guys that come along that change things forever. Back in the day, Charlie Christian would have been one…Eddie Lang, Wes Montgomery, Andrés Segovia, Chet Atkins. And Hendrix is one of those people. And he always will be. So, that's a pretty nice legacy. It doesn't need *me* to bring my influence to bear on how he will be remembered – he already is remembered for the legacy of his own stuff.

KK DOWNING: I think the way he is remembered is he was unique in every way – as a songwriter, performer, musician, and guitar player. All in one. If you asked any guitar player on the planet today, "If you could see one guitar player play a guitar..." it would be Jimi Hendrix. It's easy to use the wheel, but it's not easy to *invent* the wheel, right?

REVEREND HORTON HEAT: As the architect of modern heavy metal guitar. But also, as a blues guy. He played with Little Richard – he was more of a "blues/rock n' roll guy" than a "heavy metal guy." But he was doing wild stuff. There's some old TV footage, when you see Hendrix when he was wearing a band outfit with the other guys in the band, and immediately, you can tell it's *him*. And he's doing all this over-the-top stuff with the guitar. He was headed in that direction – even when he was a sideman.

RICHARD LLOYD: He turned the world of music on its ear – upside down, inside out, and backwards. Otherworldly. I mean, he was on this planet, but I'm not sure he was *from* this planet. He had a human body, but he was like an avatar of the guitar – a living god. I don't worship him, but he's a god – in the same way that Hindus have gods. He was an avatar of the electric guitar.

Other Books By Greg Prato

Music:

A Devil on One Shoulder and an Angel on the Other: The Story of Shannon Hoon and Blind Melon

Touched by Magic: The Tommy Bolin Story

Grunge Is Dead: The Oral History of Seattle Rock Music

No Schlock...Just Rock! (A Journalistic Journey: 2003-2008)

MTV Ruled the World: The Early Years of Music Video

The Eric Carr Story

Too High to Die: Meet the Meat Puppets

The Faith No More & Mr. Bungle Companion

Overlooked/Underappreciated: 354 Recordings That Demand Your Attention

Over the Electric Grapevine: Insight into Primus and the World of Les Claypool

Punk! Hardcore! Reggae! PMA! Bad Brains!

Iron Maiden: '80 '81

Survival of the Fittest: Heavy Metal in the 1990s

Scott Weiland: Memories of a Rock Star

German Metal Machine: Scorpions in the '70s

The Other Side of Rainbow

Shredders!: The Oral History of Speed Guitar (And More)

The Yacht Rock Book: The Oral History of the Soft, Smooth Sounds of the 60s, 70s, and 80s

100 Things Pearl Jam Fans Should Know & Do Before They Die

The 100 Greatest Rock Bassists

Long Live Queen: Rock Royalty Discuss Freddie, Brian, John & Roger

King's X: The Oral History

Facts on Tracks: Stories Behind 100 Rock Classics

Dark Black and Blue: The Soundgarden Story

Take It Off: Kiss Truly Unmasked

A Rockin' Rollin' Man: Bon Scott Remembered

Bonzo: 30 Rock Drummers Remember the Legendary John Bonham

Sports:
Sack Exchange: The Definitive Oral History of the 1980s New York Jets

Dynasty: The Oral History of the New York Islanders, 1972-1984

Just Out of Reach: The 1980s New York Yankees

The Seventh Year Stretch: New York Mets, 1977-1983

Printed in Great Britain
by Amazon

51150658R00168